STARTING OVER
STORIES OF NEW
BEGINNINGS

Eileen Doyon

Starting Over

Published by October Hill, LLC
www.unforgettablefacesandstories.com

Layout and cover design by
Kirsten Larsen Schultz | Marketing Ally
www.marketingally.net

Cover Photographs by
Fred Wehner
www.tug44.org/wild.life

Printed in the United States of America.

ISBN: 0692898646
ISBN-13: 978-0692898642

THANK YOU

I wanted to take a moment to thank a village in Upstate New York, Fort Edward. My wonderful hometown. I love you all. The people there are fabulous, and I cannot start naming names with the fear of omitting someone either by name or nickname (private joke for all in Fort Edward from aka Mitz, Mitzi, Dom, e, beanz). Growing up in a small town was a wonderful, bonding experience. The love and the meaning of "being raised by a village" still exists. I have seen everyone pull together and support, fight, love, encourage, and donate to so very many people. It warms my heart and soul. For there is where I started ......and for there comes my new beginning........

And thank you for purchasing Starting Over: Stories of New Beginnings! We are very excited about this seventh book in the Unforgettable Faces & Stories series.

Other books in the Unforgettable Faces & Stories series:
Dedications: Dads & Daughters
Keepsakes: Treasures From The Heart
Best Friends: Forever & Ever
Pet Tales: Unconditional Love
Letters To Heaven
The Second My Life Changed Forever

As we grow our community of storytellers, we would appreciate your help in getting the word out about us. Here are a few ways you can help:
- Like / share our Facebook page: www.facebook.com/ unforgettablefacesandstories
- Connect with Eileen on Linked in: www.linkedin.com/in/eileendoyon
- Please write a review on Amazon
- Send us a video testimonial.
- We love written testimonials too!

Thank you again for your support! We would love for you to participate in one of our upcoming books...YOUR story told by YOU!

CONTRIBUTORS

In line with our mission of Your Story Told by YOU, this book is written by the above contributers in their own words and style. To keep the stories true to their original submission, editing on the stories is limited.

UNFORGETTABLE FACES & STORIES

STARTING OVER
STORIES OF NEW
BEGINNINGS

Amanda Bacon

It starts off magically. The new crush, we'll call him Lyman, he says all the right things, does all the right things, courting, and showing deep affection without hesitation.

And so, it began, this man I decided to let into my life and begin an intimate relationship with, lit up when he saw me, almost making me believe I had cast a magical spell over him. The charm oozed out of him, "you're going to like me" he would say all the time with a wry grin. "I know I can get you to like me" – and I would giggle, thinking this guy is really pulling out all the stops...a long-time acquaintance who had admired me from a far. I had clearly made an impression. The stars aligned and now we could be together.

I over-looked things, like the fact his wife had *just* died. And when I say *just*, I mean that within the first month of her death we had reconnected as friends. But, because she had cheated on him in their 10+ year marriage, as he would tell you – it was miserable for at least half of it. He repeatedly shared that they fought all the time (red flag), argued in front of their son (red flag), she cheated on him (red flag), they went financially bankrupt (red flag), and he resented her for all of it (red flag), and never stopped drilling the specifics of his dissatisfaction and anger into our new-relationship.

I was direct and sincere in my concern when I questioned him about the timing of him pursing this relationship. I brought up the subject of the grief process several times, offering to wait for a few months, a year if that was what he needed. Yet, he remained steadfast in his confidence on account of the damage of his marriage, he was ready to move on and that I was the girl he'd dreamt of since he was 16 years old.

Time went on, guilt and drama seeped out of him, I tried to make it better. I tried to help me feel better too, by remaining supportive and loving. Then the horror stories of his childhood came out, and abuse that he never addressed (red flag). Everything was always someone else's fault (red flag). But it was okay I thought, because he knows when to take ownership of his missteps, I'd seen him do it.

Me? I had just come out of an extremely scary marriage, terminated when my husband left me when I was four months pregnant. He had been hiding a drug and alcohol addiction. Then mental illness consumed my ex-husband who had been made acutely aware of the treatments, yet dismissed all support, and I consequently spent the next few years trying desperately to keep my daughter safe.

So, my attention between getting back up on my feet from the loss of my marriage, giving birth to, and then fighting to keep my daughter safe, starting to become self-reliant and witnessing great success in my professional career, and then falling in love with someone who made me feel alive again, gave me a new purpose. I felt like I was the only woman in the world and I deserved all great things…and Lyman was perfect for me. So you see, I deserved him because he consistently told me that I deserved him. Which, left me very little headspace to see clearly again. It was raining red flags and I remained blinded by love under my umbrella of illusion.

Soon the "please help me with overcoming my inner demons" and "please help me raise my son", and "you have such good values" and, "I want your family as part of my family" – turned into him accusing me of over-stepping his boundaries. The push and pull and tug of war became a constant game of hot potato – I never knew which version of Lyman I was going to get. But, whenever I got the Lyman I fell in love with…everything in the world was right.

His pull was the best high in the world, and the push only wanted me to pull harder.

And let's not leave out the sex. I never ever (ever) knew sex could be like that. Every single time was so passionate, so over the top amazing. It was never just screwing with him. It was always intense, passionate, vulnerable love making that would last hours and hours…every time. We couldn't get enough of each other.

Time went on. Years went by. Our two children, who met at ages 7 years and 9 months old, formed a bond. We formed bonds with each other's children. His son, became my son. I was the one who picked him up from school, helped with homework, protected him when Lyman went into rage (red flag). I was the one his son confided in about being bullied, and told me what really scared him, and what made him happy (like dancing around the house in my high heels when his dad wasn't home). I was his safe, stable person. And Lyman loved that, until he didn't – and then once again I wouldn't know where I stood. Push, pull. Red Flag.

This man put me up on a pedestal from day one, yet without a foundation. As a result, I became easy to knock off, and then put back up. (Red flag). Each fall becoming worse than the last, and each time he put me back up on the pedestal, I believed it was all that more meaningful. Red flag.

But then almost three years into the relationship, I began recognizing my own inner voice in my head as I was with him. It was literally screaming GET OUT – RUN! RUN AWAY! HE ISN'T GOOD FOR YOU. THIS ISN'T WORKING. GO GO GO! My inner truth was taking control.

But I stayed. In hopes that he would love me, and make love to me, and make it better.

As time went by, I felt I had invested so much into him, into us, into his son and sharing my daughter with them. How could I have wasted that time? No. We had to make this work. Whatever it took. So, my grip became stronger, and he became meaner.

Until finally – after months of on and off torture – no, wait – nearly 3 years, and for nothing at all in particular – it just ended. No kindness, no thanks for the lessons learned, no I wish you the best. It just ended – and that is how it needed to end. It needed to be severed. So, I made a choice, start the New Year without him.

I never reached back for him. Ever. Months later, of course as my mother predicted, he started emailing, calling, texting. I didn't respond. This drove him mad. Interesting foot-note – it took him about 24 hours to begin dating someone else after our break-up. Yes, that hurt, but I shouldn't have been surprised because I also knew he was screwing someone hours after his wife died and pursued me just weeks later. Red flag.

Another month later I got a crazy-person-email from him, blaming me and my family for everything that went wrong between us. What came next was an actual picture of him down on his knees, begging for forgiveness. He texted that he couldn't stop crying, he still could not sleep, he was having panic attacks, and he missed me. All while he still had this new girlfriend by his side.

Back to me. I started over, suffering from the amputation of the love I had believed in. I missed him desperately. I still miss his son.

But time began to make things a little better, and I had been through worse, the fight for safety of my daughter. I practiced what I learned through that ordeal, just put one foot in front of the other. I had to untangle myself from his sickness and evaluate my role in the relationship. I had to grieve the loss of the lies that I believed. He never meant anything he said to me about our future, and I had to forgive myself for believing him. I hurt deeply over his lies, because I realized, to him - I was never worth the truth.

It was then that I broke through the mirror of illusion, and I learned how to forgive myself for loving and trusting the wrong person. I acknowledged and prided myself on offering him love and truth and commitment during our relationship. The truth ultimately became, *he did not deserve me.*

I turned my attention towards my daughter, family, friends, and career. And my life, almost overnight, changed.

I began to fall deeper in-love with my daughter. My relationship with my family – which was already very strong, became more connected, more honest – because they had been seeing what I refused to look at. My relationships with my girlfriends truly deepened, as I realize now the importance of having loving supporting women around me, because through all walks of life – we get it. We are the mothers, wives, girlfriends, divorcees, struggling and soaring. We are the ones who don't falter.

Within no time – my career, which Lyman was super competitive with (red flag) – soared in new directions I couldn't imagine.

I began to really understand what this *universal law* thing is all about. The happier I became inside, the better and clearer I was able to embrace the wonderful, meaningful things that came my way.

This does not mean I am Susie Sunshine all the time. I have bad terrible days, just like everyone else, but I don't try to mask them anymore. I let them come, so I can let them go.

I now believe in myself in a way I never have before. I believe I will not make the same mistakes with men again, and if God forbid I do find myself in a relationship with another whack-job, I will immediately remove myself, no more waiting to see if the red flags go away. THEY ARE THERE FOR A REASON. And I won't blame myself for them either.

Heartache hurts, but I learned that hurt is an opportunity for healing. My heartache is gone, and I feel closer to the magic and wonder of life and can state with pure resolution, that I am happy and free. I now know I deserve the best, and will settle for nothing less.

AMY SPILSBURY

2014 was the most challenging year of my life. I was 21 at the time and in the space of three months it felt as though my entire life had fallen apart; but this turned out to be just the beginning of an amazing journey.

It was July, the height of summer in England and everything was going great, I had a good job, I'd just moved into an apartment with my best friend and was basking in my new found freedom.

At this time I hadn't spoken to my Dad for three years due to nothing in particular, just our own stubbornness. After all these years of putting off reaching out to him because I was afraid, I'd decided it was time to call him and put all this behind us. Although I was terrified to even dial the number, I was excited to hear his voice and my mind raced with all the things I wanted to tell him.

My Step Mom answered the phone, I froze and hung up but within seconds she called me back and as she began to speak I knew exactly what she was going to say. She told me that my Dad had passed away three months ago. When I put the phone down with her I didn't know what to do; I was overcome with guilt and grief with nowhere to turn for any form of closure.

As I began to deal with these emotions I started to view my entire life differently because I felt I'd been robbed of time that I thought I had; I was angry at myself for being so complacent and it was incredibly frustrating. I vowed to never let that happen again.

Around two weeks later, my Mom came over to tell me that she was moving away to Ireland, she'd decided to sell her business and start a fresh over there. I was so shocked that I couldn't say anything for a few minutes, it was so out of the blue and also at a time where I really needed her around. My heart sank and I then felt empty and even more alone.

When I went to work the next day I realized how much I hated my job. From the outside looking in, it was great but the reality was that I couldn't handle the pressure they put on me and especially not now. The recent events in my life had really put things into perspective and I felt so disinterested with certain things. I think when you're going through such grief, all the trivial things in life become so irrelevant and it's almost frustrating to be around people who are stressed about something other than life or death.

In all the emotional chaos I was facing, I took a two week vacation to Costa Rica. I'd booked the trip almost a year ago and it came around at the most perfect time because it made me feel alive again and it also made me realize what I really wanted.

Near the end of the trip our bus pulled up to a petrol station on the side of a mountain. It was almost sunset and the view was incredible. As I looked around me at the dimming light and wild birds flying overhead, I thought to myself "You know what? I'm with nobody familiar, in a place I don't know and I'm so happy. I'm okay." I didn't want to go home. I just wanted to continue my adventure and experience more of the world! But I couldn't… I was now in thousands of pounds of debt from the trip, with no savings so I had to accept the fact that this would take some time. I decided that when I got home, I would work harder than ever to pay off my debt and save up enough money to move somewhere far away and start over. I didn't think of it as 'running away', it wasn't that. I wanted to feel excited about my life again and I knew in my heart this is what it would take.

When I got home from my trip I was dreading going back to work but also motivated to put my plan into action; however two weeks into my money saving mission I was fired. This was the third event that hit me like a ton of bricks, out of nowhere and it was so disheartening but I was not willing to give up.

I turned my sadness into a kind of anger, I became a woman on a mission, feisty and fiery! Within four days I'd secured a new job and not only did it turn out to be the most fun place I'd ever worked but it also allowed me to earn almost double my previous salary. Over the next two years I managed to pay off all my debt, save up some money and visit seven countries in the process!

These two years were frustrating at times because I'm so impatient, but I thought back to that moment at the petrol station in Costa Rica almost every day. I reminded myself how wonderful and alive I felt and that my efforts really would be worth it. I also had a repeating playback of memories in my mind of all the times my Dad had told me that intention wasn't enough, you have to take action and do it!

This time also allowed me to work out what my vision of living abroad actually looked like. I'd decided to move to China to teach English, even though I'd never been before, couldn't speak the language and had never taught before. I'd heard about people doing it and it seemed like an awesome experience, despite everyone around me thinking I was completely insane, I was more than ready to take a leap of faith.

I managed to find a teaching job with almost unbelievable ease and it all happened very quickly; I had two months to tie up all my lose ends in England and arrive in Guangzhou by August. I sold nearly everything I owned, quit my job and spent some real quality time with my family. I had an almost constant knot of fear in my stomach but I focused on the excitement - I was finally starting a new chapter.

My leaving day came around in the blink of an eye and now here I am, writing this from my apartment in Guangzhou, China. I've been here for eight months and I have no plans to return to England. China has been everything and more than I imagined it to be. I've been on some crazy adventures here and met the most incredible people who I know will be lifelong friends. I've had so many opportunities fall in my lap and I feel proud of myself because I know it was me that created this life and these circumstances.

I can also tell you with such honesty that I wake up every day feeling excited for what lies ahead, not just in my day, but in my life. I will be forever grateful for what happened in 2014 because it was the catalyst for me to chase my dream. It taught me to never put things on hold and if you want something, you'll find a way. However, most importantly I learned that I will always be okay.

ANNA ANDERSON

It's not always a bed of roses – and wow what a garden!

As we taxi down the runway on a plane heading 'home' to Nanjing from Guangzhou we reflect, as we often do, on how different our lives would be if we hadn't made the huge leap we did on 17 December 2012.

The flight attendant has just told me to turn my phone off as I began to make notes and it's the first time ever I find myself without a notebook to jot my thoughts down on. And so the first draft of this message is on the two serviettes I got given in Starbucks with my coffee, the only paper I can find in my backpack and I think of the title I have been given to write on "A New Beginning – A New Chapter in My Life"

On that day 17 December 2012, having sold everything we owned, our new life became a reality as we touched down at Lukou International Airport – the start of a whole new life in China. Neither of us had ever been to China before, we knew nobody and were unable to speak the language. Nanjing is one of the Four Great Ancient Capitals of China, not that we cared, having arrived in the middle of the day to a temperature of -1.0 degrees Celsius, a little different to the close to 25 degrees Celsius we left in Wellington around 24 hours before.

I will never forget how I felt as we landed. Our first impressions were not good! It was cold. It was dark. Everything was completely foreign (including the toilets and that's a whole other story). It was scary and I had a tonne of drugs with me having been diagnosed with pneumonia a day or so before leaving New Zealand. Not a great way to start an adventure. I remember distinctly saying to Michael that it felt more like landing in Russia (even though I have never been to Russia and have no idea what that would feel or be like arriving in Russia).

While being overtaken by a wave of excitement, I felt sick. I felt tearful. I felt like we had landed on another planet, everything was grey. The weather was overcast and foggy – grey. The buildings were concrete block – grey. There was no color on the walls within the airport – grey. The floors were like old classroom lino – grey. GREY is not my favorite color! We looked at each other wondering what the hell had we done as we walked the stark, long grey corridors to Immigration, to enter our new life.

That was over four years ago now. We are still here in Nanjing and for the most part, still loving our "new" life. Today, we've just finished a three-day speaking tour in three cities – Dongguan, Zhongshan and Jiangmen, in the south of China. While tired, I feel completely energized having spent three days speaking to audiences of around 200 people each day, on the topic of Global Communication.

And today, as we do most days, we marvel and giggle at the life we lead here in Nanjing, traveling and speaking to audiences of 3-500 people, delivering soft skills training to Multinational Corporations working with individuals and Small/Medium Enterprises expanding their global businesses through presentations and other global communication platforms. And all of this in English to audiences of Chinese people whose English levels are intermediate at best. Something we never thought we would be doing when we got married 35 years ago.

Yes, there have been many challenges and along with them, so many new learning experiences. One thing is for sure, living in China has provided us, our marriage, and our business with a whole new energy. We feel a whole lot more alive over here, dare I say it, younger, way less likely to sweat the small stuff or care so much about what others think. And to live here for an extended period of time, takes an incredible amount of flexibility, courage, and stamina.

I underestimated how much I would miss cruising into an English bookstore to simply browse, my favorite foods readily available, drinkable tap water, blue lakes, rivers and streams, western medicine, and all those little things we take for granted. I underestimated how much influence little things have on your mindset and wellbeing, like sunshine and blue sky in the midst of smog, the clean beautiful fresh smells that need to be created to enhance your inner senses, stars on a clear night sky or even the ability to inadvertently eavesdrop on everybody's conversations on a crowded train or bus, feeling connected. We are so in tune to English that our ears pick up an English conversation so easily in the midst of daily hustle bustle, even before you can find the person speaking.

And I wouldn't change it for the world. So many thought and told us that we were mad making the change, afterall we had a relatively comfortable life in New Zealand, we lived in one of the most beautiful countries in the world. Most thought we were going through a mid life crisis, well at least me with Mike was just coming along for the ride. Looking back maybe they were right and I don't believe it was a "crisis" – it was a midlife awakening (without getting all religious), awakening to what is available to all of us if we just dare to take that step out of our relative "comfort zone".

And for me the best part of the journey is that I have opened up the world to my daughters, giving them space to grow in their perspectives, become so much more accepting and adaptable and so much more open to diversity in every shape and form. For most of their childhood I talked about freedom, choice, feeling the fear and doing it anyway, they were always the first recipients of any new insights or learnings I had in my own personal development journey – now I know I'm not just talking the talk, I'm walking the walk! They know of my fears. They know of our challenges. They share in the highs and the lows and know now that anything is possible.

So that is my message to the world – anything is possible if you really want it AND it's your choice. If you don't want it be okay with that too, it's your choice. If you do want it, then get out and make it happen, don't give into complacency and comfort, build the courage and confidence to create the life you desire – ups and downs and everything in between. Get over your excuses. Age, Nationality, Education, Background – none of these matter. Each and every one of us has the ability to create their own journey and enjoy every day to the fullest (whatever that means for you)!

We have achieved so much coming here, done so many things we would have never even attempted in New Zealand, we have created a new way of life, a global business, filled with so many new opportunities, extending our whanau globally and truly creating a whole new perspective on life, on the world and on the wonderful diversity of people within. There is so much more out there to see and do – bring it on world!

"Life should not be a journey to the grave with the intention of arriving safely in an attractive and well-preserved body, but rather to skid in sideways, champagne in one hand, strawberries in the other, body thoroughly used up, totally worn out, and screaming... WOO HOO, WHAT A RIDE" -Kate Langdon

Photos shown: First week in Nanjing – below zero temperatures
This was basically the size of our room; Kids visiting for a winter in China;
Traveling and training; Family working together in China – team work

Anne Pendergrass

It was the end of the life I cherished. My husband, Jack, lay dying in the bed in front of me. The pain and suffering he endured was a testimony to the love he had for me and our marriage until he drew his final breath.

We were always close and had the kind of marriage that dreams are made of. Although he didn't own a suit of shining armor or a white horse, he always made me feel like I was the center of his world. He was not just my husband but my best friend, my lover and my soul mate. There wasn't anything in the world we wouldn't do for each other and the depth of those feelings made losing him unbearable.

When he was first diagnosed with cancer five months earlier, I was devastated. He kept telling me that no matter what, he could make it through the treatments. He said he was strong and had no intention of letting something like this tear us apart. Although I cried everyday, he remained strong emotionally and did everything he could to reassure me that we'd get through this together and end up having the life we just started living. He only asked that I not give up on him.

Fast forward five months later as we stood in his hospital room, his Hospice caretaker told me that his suffering would continue unless I was willing to help let him go. She proceeded to tell me that in one of their many conversations, Jack told her about our love and the life we had carved out for ourselves. She told me that there was nothing in the world that meant more to him than our life together and he was trying very hard to hold on to it. Unless I was willing to tell him it was okay to stop fighting, this suffering could go on indefinitely.

With a heavy heart, I sat next to his bed and spoke quietly into his ear telling him it was okay to let go. He had been a wonderful husband and had given me more in five years than I ever dreamed possible. It was okay to go, but be sure to wait for me in heaven. He expired within ten minutes holding my hand. I am still bothered by the guilt I carried for so long for having broken my promise to him. I've always been afraid he thought I gave up on him. Consequently, my grieving process did not take the normal route.

I became extremely depressed and anorexic. Having been raised a Catholic, I knew suicide was a mortal sin and couldn't do that or I'd never get to see Jack again. I rationalized in my clouded mind that I wouldn't do anything to actively take my own life, but I did have the power to passively let it happen by not eating. The thought of food gave me nausea anyway. I too was dying a slow death. But it was the only way to be with Jack again.

Family and friends were afraid of what was happening to me and as a result, I spent more time with the medical profession than I care to admit. I was able to continue working but my supervisor, Tom, who was also my friend, made my job contingent on seeking professional help. Otherwise, I would no longer be able to continue in my position. He provided a name and phone number and I called that week.

As the months went by, my anorexic condition worsened along with many of the side effects that went with it. My supervisor traveled frequently for his job and soon was promoted to a new position. We rarely saw each other after that. However, whenever he came home, he would always call to check on me and take me to lunch. Since Tom had been Jack's friend as well as mine, he seemed to take on the responsibility of making sure I was going to make it through this downward spiral which became all consuming. At times, it appeared that feeding me became Tom's mission in life.

As the months turned into years, our friendship and affection for each other deepened. I started gaining the weight I had lost the year following Jack's death. It was a slow and difficult process but Tom stayed by my side throughout my recovery. He was strong, steady, always dependable, affectionate and loving. It became impossible not to fall in love with someone who so freely gave of himself and did whatever it took to make sure I was back on track.

Fifteen years ago, Tom and I were married. He taught me how to love and trust again. Our life together hasn't always been smooth sailing, as in any marriage, but the deep and abiding love and respect we have for each other has always been the cornerstone of our life together.

Some people never get to experience true love and friendship in a marriage. I have been blessed to have it happen to me twice in life. I'll never know what I did in my life to deserve such happiness but being willing to take a chance and start over has made all the difference.

April McGinnis

Changing My Stars

My life occurrences have not been significantly different than what most people experience in the course of their life. I can expound on particulars but I am not certain that my story would be any different than what the average person has to share. I see life as ever changing, starting over, and l have realized that change can be growth and that fear is fleeting.

My personal narrative hasn't always been a positive one but I am a work in process. My authentic self is still evolving, my legacy is yet somewhat undefined and my journey is still in motion. There are many choices to make, paths to be taken, people to encounter, obstacles to overcome and many open doors to enter.

Life is a state of constant change and starting over with new beginnings. Nothing remains the same, unavoidably nature takes its course or totally unexpected change happens or a decision is made that has an impact that we hope has the predictable expected outcome. A life changing moment is always on the verge of happening and I have found that I experience some form of change daily. I have realized it is all in how I will accept or reject that moment and the lesson I can learn from the circumstance, no matter how pivotal or seemingly pointless it may be. Change hasn't always been easy for me. In fact, I still don't always appreciate it in the moment but eventually I come around, I find some understanding, and I set out to make the best of it. I try to think of the big picture. Although I often initially resist change, I eventually lean into it and allow my life to just flow.

I realized at an early age that if I was going to survive the very unstable and frightening life I was forced to live at that time, that I needed to change my stars; I would learn that I would need to do it continuously. Actually, I was around five years old when I first decided that my destiny would not be a place void of love, light, safety and acceptance. However, as a child there isn't a lot that can be done to change your life other than to depend on others and to wait. Self-awareness has always been my friend, although, to be honest, not always present, but once discovered and timely rediscovered, it has become one of my greatest assets as well. How I perceived my life at that early age created the foundation for how I want to walk my path; that early observation allows me to embrace change and to seize opportunities that will propel me forward no matter how my life is viewed at the moment by me or those around me.

My journey has presented many instances that have caused me to detour from but also brought me closer to my true nature, and has eventually allowed me to accept and at times, relentlessly pursue changes. There have been life defining events that have left me weak and wounded, strong and joyful. My daily life is about excelling, about realizing that every single occurrence brings me to another path on my journey and an opportunity to evolve, adapt and walk in wisdom and truth as changes occur.

Everything has a season. In the last few years I have experienced some drastic changes, some I instigated in order to move onward in my life, some were forced upon me without my consent and some, just random events. I lost my mother, experienced the end of a 20 year marriage, changed jobs twice, decided to change my social circle, discovered a soul mate, sent my son off to the US Navy and watched my daughter blossom into a delightful young women.

Although there have been the typical life altering events, there isn't one that has absolutely changed me more than another. Being pregnant and experiencing the birth of a baby girl and then a few years later, a baby boy, set my heart ablaze and my life has certainly never been the same. Experiencing the death of my mother brought the realization that my life is much more fragile than I had ever considered. These were profound moments and brought life full circle. Still, all of these changes, no matter how beautiful or devastating, are only part of life that has transformed me. The everyday occurrences and choices that are left unperceived by the world, these are the moments that are defining who I am. These are the moments that create my life.

Changes are often disguised as painful wounds or rejections but they too have been just what I needed when I least expected it. Life can be a series of sepia tone still pictures but the changes that I seek, that I survive, that I revel in, those are what transforms my life into a vibrant, shiny picture that captures the essence of me. I just have to remember to look through the positive lenses of perspective and be reminded that change is part of my journey. Without change, there would be no progress, no beginnings and no endings.

There is opportunity in change. When so much is shifting around me, when my life is altered and unpredictable, it is essential to recall that change is inevitable and often times, good and necessary. My stars are destined, still in the destiny, I have some control. I have the ability to control my reactions to the random, or foreseeable and impermanent changes that life brings. In an instant, everything can change, how we choose to accept it or fight it won't even bother to define what change is capable of; it is glorious and frightening and it is unavoidable. I have the choice to shine bright in the instance of change or to hide in a dark corner. I will always find a way to shine bright.

Life doesn't have a set of directions, there is no manual with an index telling us which chapter and page to reference. We are constantly on the verge of changing, it takes one decision no matter how slight or well thought out to change our course. It takes one casual occurrence that we have no real control over to set us on a path that can impact us and even those closest to us. The question is, what we will do to make the impact of the change as positive as we can and to lend its outcome to the success and fulfillment of the life we are living now.

Progress is impossible without change, and those who cannot change their minds cannot change anything. - George Bernard Shaw

BARBARA MARCHETTI

As a mother of one and a wife, the most poignant life-changing event occurred seven years ago when my son, now almost 19, entered prep school in 6th grade at the age of 12.

Three weeks into my son's "new school" he started experiencing symptoms that would initially last for an hour and over the course of a couple of weeks escalated up to several hours a day, every day. It started with the metallic taste in his mouth which would lead to uncontrollable "cyclic" vomiting along with excruciating pain in both his head and abdomen. Every day that we departed on the 35 mile drive to school, I could feel the dread creep in as I held my breath, praying that today would be a "symptom" free day. For almost 7 months, my son experienced these dreadful symptoms daily both in my car and in the school nurse's office. I watched my sweet, brave, little boy endure seven months of E.R. visits, invasive testing and numerous exams by neuro docs. Although grateful that he was not diagnosed with a life-threatening illness, the crushing blow came to us when told that his symptoms were the result of one thing: anxiety. Anxiety to do everything well, to please his teachers, his coaches and yes, his parents. Heartbreaking. We/I were/was to blame. I took my competitive drive in the business world, in the boardroom, and transferred that to my son. Plain and simple. Our lofty expectations and standards were too much for him to bear. How could I have done this to my beautiful child?

Once diagnosed and lined up with the proper therapy, we now had to face the challenge of helping him catch up on the work he missed over 30 days of absences. He was determined to graduate from 6th grade so he could stay with his friends. Despite working with tutors 7 days per week while attending classes and seeing a CBT therapist who practiced hypnotherapy, he managed to pull it all together without suffering anymore symptoms by the 4th quarter of 6th grade. He did it because he wanted to not because we forced him to do so.

Fast forward 7 years later: tomorrow he walks the halls of that prep school for the final time. He graduates in a week and will start his new life at his first choice, Wheaton College, where he was recruited to swim. As the Captain of his Varsity Swim team at prep school, league MVP, school record breaker and

All-star for the past 4 years, my son proudly accepted his award yesterday as one of 3 seniors who had perfect attendance throughout his high school years. Truth be told…he has had perfect attendance there since the 4th quarter of 6th grade!

My son showed me that he could have "balance" with both school and swim but on his own terms, not mine, without being sleep deprived, without caffeine, without hysteria. Happy, healthy, pushing himself to do well but not consumed with being better than everyone else…I've learned a lot from him.

BECKY ROY

Farmers' Daughter

How do you repay those who gave you life? How do you know if they know how much you loved them? How do you know **how** to begin your life without them, and not feel guilty, or cry? All of us will ask these questions at some point in our lives. While they themselves are not easy to answer, neither is the path we travel to find ourselves asking them.

My story isn't exceptional, but I can say that my journey through loss and grief began three and a half years ago when we realized that my mother had Early Onset Dementia. My mother died peacefully, I think, last October, but I lost her long before that.

My parents would have been married 65 years last June. They had lived their lives at the family farm for all those years. Dad loved cows. He grew up with Jerseys and Guernseys, both known for their fat-rich milk. He changed to Herefords, because they were"pretty in the pasture", and were a bit lower in maintenance. He thought he would like to raise his own beef…..but he didn't have the heart to butcher more than one or two.

Mum's passion was gardening. Her flowers were the envy of all who drove by their house. She tried her hand at many varieties, and succeeded in creating a yard of beauty, the air filled with the heady scents of lilacs, mock orange, peonies, and iris, and more.

Her vegetable garden was always bountiful, as they are likely to be if you are good with dirt, and she had much to share with family, neighbors, and friends. She was most happy when she was on her knees, digging in the soil, in the warm sun, making things grow. In early years of married life, she and my grandmother canned, froze, pickled, "putting food by", which fed us all through the long Maine winters. They worked **so** hard, but they were proud and happy to do it!

In the spring of 2012 Mum fell backwards down the cellar stairs, hitting the back of her head on the concrete floor. She was home alone. She was unconscious for a short time. When she regained consciousness, she managed to crawl up the stairs, and called my great aunt, who lived next door. Fortunately, my cousin was visiting her, and he had his friend with him, who happened to be a retired ER doctor. They ran to my parents' house, to find Mum covered in blood, somewhat incoherent, and crying. The doctor checked her vitals and made sure nothing felt broken. By that time Dad returned home to find them all in the kitchen, on the floor. I got a call from my cousin, telling me Mum had fallen, injured her head, and was on her way to the ER.

Her injury was a very large hematoma which covered the entire back of her head. She regained memory of some of the accident, but was never sure of all the details. We were lucky, and she was soon back doing the things she loved. She started to forget things. She would become confused. She was unsteady on her feet. She started losing weight. Drastically. Yet she always passed the cognitive tests at the doctor's office.

She forgot how to cook. She forgot what time of day it was. She didn't know who I was when I called her. OH MY GOD! She started talking about all her children and how difficult it was to raise them. She had two. And we were adults and we were doing well.

Mum had the best guardian angel.....my Dad. She couldn't cook. No problem! He would take her out for lunch most days. She would take a little nap in the afternoon, wake up, and be angry that he let her sleep through the night in her chair! She would get up and fix toast and coffee, because she thought it was morning. It was really supper time. Dad never told us how bad she was.

One night the phone rang at 2:00 in the morning. Dad. He thought he might be having a stroke. He wanted me to call 911 and come right over. When I got there Mum didn't know what was happening. Dad told her to get dressed, and she pulled a vest on over her nightgown, and said she **was** dressed. He told me not to go to the hospital until I got my brother to come stay with Mum. She wasn't safe to be alone. **Not safe!**

Dad was diagnosed with vertigo. A severe case of vertigo. Common cause? Stress. There really isn't much for treatment of vertigo. Medication can help quell the symptoms, but the dizziness can be so bad that it makes you vomit to move.

One day after I got home from work, Dad called and asked me to meet him and Mum at the ER. Mum had been sick with vomiting and diarrhea for 2 days, and he was worried. I called my brother and his wife, and we all met at the hospital. Mum had a small bowel obstruction. We were told that it could resolve itself, but she couldn't have any solid food until the next day. She was sent home. When she got home she was hungry and made some toast and tea. Dad was frantic.

The next morning, she still was having diarrhea and severe abdominal pain. We went back to the ER. At the end of our road, my mother looked around and said, "I probably will never see this again".

That morning, Mum had emergent surgery to correct the obstruction in her small bowel. While she was in recovery, the surgeon came to talk with us. She said that apparently the obstruction **had** corrected itself, and she found no evidence of obstruction or disease. The surgeon apologized. She felt the surgery had not been necessary, even though the CT scan from the previous night clearly showed the obstruction. I'm sure she was concerned about a lawsuit, but we had no intention of suing. She was doing her job, as were we.

Mum spent a few days in the hospital, and was sent for rehab at a local nursing home. I knew I had to prepare my Dad for the turn their lives were going to take. I knew I had to become their voice, and advocate what was best for them both. I knew that by doing these things, I faced the risk of anger and resentment from them both. I knew Mum would not go home. It was April 11, 2014.

Her decline was completely devastating to our family. She was engulfed in the dark cloud of Alzheimer's, and we had to learn to be thankful for the moments of recognition that shone through.

Dad went to the nursing home every single day. He would sit with her all morning until lunch, holding her hand, and he would cry. The tears flowed so easily. The nurses felt his heartbreak, and they helped him so much with kindness. He still had terrible bouts with vertigo, and if he couldn't go see Mum, I would get a call from a nurse, checking on him.

I would go see her at supper time, after I got out of work. Often, my brother would join me there. She still knew us most of the time, but her personality was not Mum's. She lived in a different time. She hallucinated. She thought she and Dad had an apartment, and that Dad had another woman, because he didn't come home at night. She told me sometimes a man came in her bed at night. She begged us to take her home. We told her she wasn't safe at home.

By August, my Mother was in a wheelchair, wasn't eating, or talking, or focusing. I was still going to see her every night. I would try to get her to eat. ANYTHING. I would try to carry on a one-sided conversation, hoping that she would hear something that she would respond to. I would go to my car and cry. And then I would go home to my husband and try to fix a meal and have a normal life.

As Mum declined, so did Dad. He had never lived alone. Never prepared meals, never done much inside the house. I taught him to use the microwave. I cooked for him, and took it to him. My sister-in-law did the same. We started to settle into a different life.....one without Mum, as we knew her, and one that involved watching over Dad.

We continued this cycle for two years. Then Dad got sick. He had two heart attacks, brain surgery, and interstitial lung disease in his lifetime. The brain surgery, and one heart attack, as well as interstitial lung disease had occurred before Mum went to the nursing home. A second heart attack came in July 2014. He had a quick recovery, and resumed his daily visits to see Mum and "the girls", as he affectionately called the nurses. In June 2016, he started to get very weak, and tired. He thought it was allergies, because he was short of breath. That was nothing new for him, though. After a trip to the ER, he was admitted to the hospital with a severe and aggressive lung infection. Antibiotics were not stopping it. We knew he would not survive.

I cry as I put this on paper. My Dad died on June 20, 2016. My brother, his wife, my husband, and my three closest friends, as well as our special hospice team, all said good bye to the hard, yet soft man, who was the most dedicated husband and father there ever was. I held my hand on his heart and told him we were going to miss him, but he needed to go to the place where he was no longer in pain. I felt my own heart crack when he took his last breath.

At his graveside service, I read something that I had written, and when I saw all the people there to support my family, and pay respects to our father,

I was most grateful. Grateful for my family, my friends, my father. I had become so close to him in the last two and a half years. I did not know how life could continue without him.

Mum continued to fight her battle, without Dad, for four more months. She finally joined him October 23, 2016. We had music playing for her, and I selected a big band era CD. I stroked her face, held her hand and told how very much I loved her. Then I said, "It's time for you to go dancing, Mum". I went home to be with my husband, and was just sitting down to dinner when the phone rang. The voice on the other end of the line told me she was gone.

At the same time we were going through the slow agony of losing my mother, my brother was diagnosed with esophageal cancer, and while his prognosis was good, he had a long battle of treatment that he had to complete. He suffered terribly though all of it.

We also lost my brother-in-law to lung cancer. He was a sweet, big guy, who lived the best years of his life in his last 18 months.

I have learned the pain of great loss. My heart is an open heart, in that it feels everything. I do believe that God intended for me to be the voice of strength and reason, in an unreasonable situation. I cry very easily now. I also laugh freely, because I know real joy, due to the pain in my life. I know when to allow time for me. I am lucky because I have a circle of loving, supportive friends, who helped me through the dark days. My husband is my rock. He kept me strong, and helped me fight through all the legalities of holding on to 250 acres of land, and my parents' home. He loved me fiercely.

I have to believe that Mum and Dad are proud of how I helped facilitate completion of their last wishes. My brother's family will have their house and some acreage. My husband and I will have the remaining acreage, most of which is woodland. We plan to be good stewards of this land, and take care of those woods.

My husband and I built a home on land that was deeded to us by Mum and Dad. Together, with my parents, we planted 200 Christmas trees in one of the fields. The planting of the trees led to the building of a new home. It is our piece of paradise, and we treasure it every single day.

The trees are what I farm. Being the daughter of farmers, I feel it is my destiny to continue to live close to the land, and appreciate all that nature has to show us, and give us.

I have learned that love doesn't always heal us, but it helps. So does faith. Not just faith in God, but in ourselves, our family, our friends. And trust. We have to trust that we **are** doing the very best that we can, given our special circumstances.

Thank you, to my wonderful parents for giving me life, and for nurturing me and supporting me my entire life. I wish that I had been a better daughter in my younger years, but maybe I made up for that in their last years. When I look out over the land behind my house, I see them everywhere. I feel them with me always. They know how great my love is for them. I know it is time for healing, and for moving forward, and living life, again. It will just be different.

BECKY ROY

Heart Collector

It began in my thirties, after going through a divorce, and feeling very empty inside. A friend gave me a photo book of hearts, to aid in the healing of my own broken heart. And I must say that it helped. A lot. I can't really explain how it worked, but maybe it distracted me in such a way that allowed my focus to change from the great sadness I felt at where I was in life, to feeling a warmth start to kindle whenever I saw a heart. That first book of hearts was just the beginning of looking for them everywhere…in nature, in design, in everything! Hearts were all around me!

People started buying me jewelry with hearts, clothes with hearts, home décor with hearts. I doodled hearts, but then, I think I always had. I didn't know of anyone else who treasured these wonderful shapes as much as I! Hearts became my Zen!

The thirties for me were very difficult. My life had come to a crossroads, and I needed to figure out which road would make me happy. The ending of a marriage, even though it was unhappy, left me filled with shame because I was the only one in my family to get a divorce. I felt as though I had dishonored my family. I felt betrayal, because I had tried so hard to make the marriage work, but finally realized I was the only one trying. I felt so ashamed that I just wanted to curl up and die. I didn't want to cry myself to sleep anymore, and I didn't want to be strong anymore. I just wanted to die. But I didn't. I knew that either my parents would find me, or my best friend would find me. Knowing that I would leave that picture in their memories was enough for me to stumble along.

I did not have a lot of friends, but the few I had, were steadfast in their efforts to help me stay focused on getting emotionally healthy. I was mistrustful of men. I did not want to be lied to or hurt again. I wanted companionship and friendship, but nothing more. For most men, that is not the least bit appealing. At this point in time, I did not believe that I could live my life without someone in it. I was very lonely and deeply depressed.

I worked in retail management, which was low paying, dead end, and unrewarding, to say the least. I decided it was time to improve myself by going to college, when I was closing down the third store I had worked in. I asked my parents if I could move back home with them while I went to school. They agreed. That allowed me to go to school full time, and work nearly full time, and not worry about paying rent and expenses. But to move in with my parents at 32 was not easy. Not easy for any of us!

I discovered that I loved the challenge of being a college student ….in my thirties! As in high school, I had to study very hard to do well. Days off from work were spent in classes, and studying. There was not any time left for a social life. Even though I was happy pursuing an education, I continued to feel extreme loneliness. I longed for some single friends to do things with. I dated a little, but my schedule didn't allow much time for it. I also was at the point where I didn't want to settle, and I didn't want a one night stand. My search for the elusive heart gave me hope, though, and I continued my ever constant quest for it!

As I neared graduation, I became hopeful that good things were coming. I graduated with honors, and was deeply proud of my accomplishment. I felt SMART! My confidence had improved, and I liked the woman I was becoming.

This time was a real turning point for me. I still longed for someone to share my life with, but I also knew that if it didn't happen, I would be ok on my own. And this was when I met my husband! My heart was open….and ready for love!

We met through mutual friends, and had gone to school together as kids. Our lives had taken quite different paths. Our first date was a coffee date. We talked for hours. And we talked on the phone every night those first weeks. Before we realized it, we had fallen in love. For the first time ever, a man loved me for who I was, and that feeling was so incredible!!

Miriam Webster defines the heart as the central or innermost part of something. I know that my heart is my whole being. My heart, has led me through my life. Perhaps that is why I was so drawn to the wonderful shape of the heart. It is the symbol of the innermost feelings of us all. It is what makes us who we are. It is, in fact, what makes us tick.

Through the years, I have found others who are collectors of hearts. We share a common thread, weaving golden strands of warmth and happiness into our ordinary lives, making us feel extraordinary. I notice that many of us who collect are creative, and perhaps this is what allows us to see the hearts of nature, and help us recreate these special forms in our own artwork.

It's amazing to be walking on a path and find a heart rock, or see a clump of tiny white flowers in the shape of a heart. Heart rocks, themselves are a special Phenom. In my travels I have seen hearts displayed on front porches, in gardens, in walkways, and even in front steps! To see them, ALWAYS makes me smile, and I must take a picture to have for a keepsake.

Life gets complicated at times. We have so many responsibilities that we don't look for pleasure in the simple things. Our careers, our families, our social commitments......they all fill the spaces in our lives. We forget that our souls need to be nurtured in order to remain healthy. If we don't keep our spirits healthy, we will shrivel up and become empty of feeling. We can't allow that to happen!

Since the passing of my parents last year, I have decided that I am going to reinvent myself, by incorporating more of my creations into my life, as well as others. I knit, sew, make jewelry, and cards and take photos. One constant in my pieces is the heart. It has become my signature because it makes me happy, in creating things, and also spreading the love they seem to invoke.

I think that because of my collecting of hearts, I am more open to feelings, memories, and the beyond…..maybe God…..and because I am always looking for them, I find them! And finding them makes my own heart happy! Very happy!

BILL GURNON

The Choice

Choosing to give college a second chance changed my life.

~ ~ ~

I am the oldest of five children. For many of my formative years we lived in Massachusetts, near my dad's parents. We were a fairly normal family, so far as I could tell. We struggled financially but as a kid, I didn't know enough to care. I was happy. I lacked only one thing, a dog.

I couldn't have a dog because my brother Jimmy had severe allergies and life-threatening asthma. It seemed as though he was allergic to everything including peanut butter, fresh air and, yes, dogs. He was hospitalized once or twice every year. My parents had no health insurance and Dad worked two jobs to pay for his care.

Our meals were simple and basic – potatoes, meatloaf, lima beans and the like. We never ate out.

We didn't take vacations either. Two or three times a summer we'd go to the beach on a Sunday afternoon, or take the 45-minute drive to visit the history center at Plymouth Rock. We'd lean over the fence protecting Plymouth Rock and spit on it. We meant no disrespect. It was just something kids do. After spending the afternoon seeing the Pilgrim actors, we'd drive back home and watch *The Lawrence Welk Show* on TV. Exciting stuff.

Life was a challenge for my parents. They argued. Dad wasn't healthy and he lost his job. Jimmy wasn't getting any better. In hopes of starting over, we moved to Minnesota, where Mom's parents lived.

Minnesota didn't help. My parents continued to struggle. And, they didn't suffer in silence. They'd say things like, "The only luck we'll ever have is bad luck" or, "If the worst can happen, it will." Statements like these were spoken often. In my child's brain, I thought this was normal. But, their continued pessimism hovered over my happiness like a dark cloud and I slowly began to believe hardship was my fate.

As a teenager entering middle school, I started taking on the victim role modeled by my parents. Struggle became a part of my life. I wanted to be in sports but wasn't good enough. Two tough guys with slicked-back Elvis hair bullied me nearly everyday. Jimmy and I argued all the time – I was jealous of all the attention he was getting. Like my parents, I started believing that I didn't deserve to have anything good and that happiness was not my birthright. I had become a victim. My parents weren't at fault. Their belief system was shaped by the tough times of The Great Depression and I respect them for their accomplishments.

After high school, I went to college, but it didn't work out well. I was too distracted by my girl friend and didn't spend enough time on studies. My grades weren't good. I got my first 'D' ever, so I quit after just one term.

Lacking any desire to continue with college, I took the postal exam and became a US Postal Service mail handler. Surely, this would be my ticket to happiness. The job paid well and the fringe benefits were great. But, the work turned out to be dreadfully boring and I didn't connect with my co-workers. So, I gave up my 'dream' job and decided to return to college. A friend suggested a school out of state; he said it was "easy" to get good grades there.

I tried it that summer and, he was right! I did get better grades, so I decided to stay.

And, this is where my new beginning started.

After six months of commuting to this Wisconsin college from St. Paul, MN, I decided to move onto the campus, away from the victim mentality of my parents. In my second year, I found myself in a dorm filled with students who believed they could create their own good luck. This was unheard of in my world. But, I saw them make it happen every day. They lived life to the fullest and the fullest came to them. It's not that they had more money, most didn't. It's not that they were smarter than me, they weren't. And, it's probably not because they grew up in Wisconsin. There are no specific examples I can cite. Yes, bad things happened. However, those things weren't seen as obstacles, they were seen as inconveniences. They chose not to let bad things get in their way. The difference between them and my parents was their attitude.

Observing how my new friends responded to life taught me that staying under the cloud that kept my parents in the shadows was optional. My friends modeled optimism. No longer did I have to be a victim. I had a choice.

One of my choices was to take a philosophy class. The professor was rude, arrogant and demanding. I loved it. His classes were engaging and interesting. However, my first paper was marked "See Me." I was terrified. In his office, he said, "Mr. Gurnon, you can do better." I took that as a compliment and tried harder; my next paper earned an A+. Choosing to accept his challenge paid off.

Now in my third year of college and feeling quite confident, I chose to speak to a physics professor whom I thought could make his class more interesting and informative – a gutsy move for a lowly undergraduate. He politely listened but completely ignored my suggestions. His lectures were a waste of time; I was learning nothing. So, I quit the class before the mid-term exam. I expected to get a failing grade, but didn't care. Surprisingly, I passed the class! Choosing to stand up for my beliefs didn't end in dire consequences.

As I started making more affirmative choices, I gained control over my life. I was no longer a victim. I could shape each day by choosing my attitude, regardless of what's going on around me. Will I choose to be depressed? Will I choose to be angry? Will I choose to be happy? If you had to make one of those choices, which would you select? It's a no-brainer, right?

It was a no-brainer for me, too. Choosing happiness was not only easier, it was more pleasant.

My new beginning had begun, thanks to that simple decision to give college one more try. Learning that we have a choice as to how we view life was the single, most important lesson I learned in college. Being grateful is the second.

Today, optimism and good choices have blessed me with a happiness I never dreamed possible. I am healthy. Good friends, beautiful music, successful children and a loving wife surround me. I live in a home that's perfectly suited for my family and my five-acre yard (farmland on which I chose to plant over 2000 trees) has become a forest filled with deer, owls, birds and other wildlife. I have much to be thankful for.

And, while I still don't have a dog, I do have a cat. Peanut's the best furry friend I've ever had.

Every day is a new beginning. And each day starts with a choice.

Life is good.

Bill Gurnon is author of *The Story Collector* and *The Story Bridge*. His website is: Story-Booker.com

BONNIE GROESSL

There Are No Accidents

It was 2009 and things were really going along pretty well in my life. I was happily married (and still am), my kids were grown, and I was busy in my private practice as a holistic nurse practitioner. Looking back, perhaps I was a bit too busy. My thoughts mostly centered on work and getting everything done. I didn't take much time to play, but life was good and I was happy.

Then, in July of 2009, my life took a detour.

It was midnight and my husband, Mike, and I were driving the highway speed limit of 65 mph. As we approached a rural intersection, the driver of a large pick-up truck failed to stop at a stop sign and drove directly into our path. We didn't have time to swerve. Upon impact, my head hit the passenger-side window hard. Despite the seat belts and air bags, I was knocked unconscious and remained in a coma for about three days. I feel blessed that medical help arrived quickly. (image 1)

My friends and family members talked to me as I lay unconscious in my hospital bed. They held my hand, prayed and waited for signs that I was waking up. I believe I heard them talking to me, because as I regained consciousness a few days later, I knew we had been in an accident.

Initially, I couldn't walk or feed myself. It's as if my brain couldn't remember how to perform these simple tasks. I had difficulty understanding conversations and felt like the world was in slow motion. I couldn't remember phone numbers, the name of the president, what day it was, or even where we lived. I had trouble recognizing words and images. However, I could remember my loved ones.

A friend started a CaringBridge website on my behalf. It helped distant family and friends stay posted on my progress, and many people sent me prayers and messages of good thoughts and love. Loved ones at the hospital read the notes posted on the site to me. Even though my brain didn't function well, I understood what they were reading.

Despite that early inability to walk, I quickly graduated from a wheelchair to a walker to walking with assistance. I had to relearn how to move my body and maintain my balance. I wasn't able to feed myself, but my husband tells me it wasn't long before I just grabbed the fork from him and tried. I wasn't very coordinated at first. I'm right-handed and my right side was not working well because the injury was mainly to the left side of my brain. Intensive physical, occupational and speech therapy began as soon as I regained consciousness. If I wasn't in therapy, I was sleeping, and vice versa. My brain needed to rest in order to heal.

With therapy, love, prayers, persistence and lots of help, my recovery was nothing short of miraculous. My homework consisted of "brain exercises" that I did several times a day. I even did simple math problems in my head while in the shower each day.

Looking back, I realize having the memory loss was a blessing. I couldn't comprehend how bad my situation was, and if I had, I know it would have been even more difficult for me. Losing your memory of traumatic period can be a very protective mechanism. I think I would have been frustrated with myself had I realized how little I could do at first. I think the memory loss was the universe's way of caring for me.

The experience I had during my recovery was beyond the feeling of being loved and cared for by other people. It was as if something greater was providing that sense of comfort, security, hope and well-being. I believe it was God and the angels supporting me. It was a feeling of peace like I had never before experienced. I truly believed everything would work out. I was able to be discharged from the hospital in time to attend my husband's book signing event just 13 days later. (image 2)

Just six weeks after the crash, I took my driving test again and passed – a requirement for people with brain injuries. I felt well enough to return to my practice on a very limited basis. It took me at least a year to feel completely normal again. My brain continues to improve daily as I continue to challenge myself and create new pathways in my brain.

I really don't remember having any negative thoughts about the accident or my injuries. I was never upset with the kids who were driving the truck that night, and was thankful they were not hurt badly. I felt at peace during the healing process and therapy. For my entire adult life, I have struggled with patience and maybe that was my lesson here. I certainly had the opportunity to practice it! I had faith I would get my life back and things would be just as they were or even better. As I was recovering, I spent time imagining that I had already healed, feeling appreciation.

I have totally reinvented the work I do since the accident. Today, I help people share their message through podcasting and publishing. We all have a message to share and our song should not go unsung.

I often stop and notice the simple things around me, and I feel so immensely blessed that I am here to enjoy my life. Gratitude is at a whole new level each day. Mike and I realize that life is too short, so we spend time on Kauai every year now. (image 3)

I believe anyone can have these feelings if they choose. We can all have the feeling of joy and excitement for each day. Sometimes it takes a traumatic life event to feel that level of peace and joy every day, but it doesn't have to be that extreme. I believe there is a reason I survived and got a second chance at life. I always say, "there are no accidents."

I practice meditation, and have for several years. In meditation, we can access that inner guidance we all have. If we are still enough, we can hear the answers to questions we ask. One day I asked why I survived and recovered so well. The answer that came to me was simple: I had to prove it could be done; not just for me, but to inspire and give hope to others.

There have been many lessons and blessings from my accident. The biggest blessing was experiencing the power of prayer, love and positive energy from so many people, as well as my own positive thoughts. I have always been mindful of the tremendous healing power within each of us, and now I have first-hand experience.

My recovery was nothing short of remarkable, and I am thankful every day for my life. I know I am not alone. I have read countless stories of people who survived the odds against cancer, terrible accidents and other life-threatening events. I am honored to be among them. (image 4)

"I always say, there are no accidents, even our car accident wasn't really an accident. It was what I was meant to experience to bring me to who I am today."

You can learn more or connect with Bonnie at http://bonniegroessl.com

CHASE COLEMAN

It started when I received my first car from my parents, Christmas of 2011. I was home (Atlanta, GA) and my parents told me that my one caveat for having a car was that I needed to get a job. I was 16 at the time and all I wanted to do was get a job that I believed I could grow in long term.

After many many interviews, I end up landing a job as a barista at Starbucks! From day 1, I told my store manager that my goal was to move into the corporate office after I graduate high school and to work for the greater enterprise.

I left for college in August of 2012 and changed my mind on what I wanted to do many times throughout college. I started off as a biology major and changed my major 7 times before I ended up on marketing. It took many interviews for internships and getting turned down by all major companies that lit a fire within myself. I was constantly thinking, "These companies think I'm not good enough for them, so I'm going to show them."

I networked on LinkedIn like it was my job. Doing nothing but sending out emails and introducing myself to senior leaders around the country, hoping someone would give me a chance. Luckily, I ended up networking with many leaders throughout Starbucks. Even after networking with some leaders at Starbucks, I got denied from their internship program. I didn't give up there though, I still wanted to be working for Starbucks, so I worked even harder and ended up applying for a full-time role. After many interviews and a spontaneous flight to Seattle, I ended up landing a full time role with Starbucks.

I moved less than a week after college graduation from Florida to Seattle. The opportunity to work for such a great brand and get my career started off on the right foot was enough for me to start over again. I realized that if I want to move forward in my career and continue to grow as an individual that I had to take this leap of faith. Move to a place that is very different from my "home", a place where I know absolutely no one, make new friends, and start my life in a brand new city to me. It was a scary feeling at first – I cried to my friends as I left because one thing I was sure of – life is going to be different from here on.

I have learned so many lessons to this date after living in Seattle by myself for over a year now. First, taking a leap of faith is important for self-growth. Being able to live in an uncomfortable situation where you know absolutely no one and where everything is quite different has taught me about who I am as a person. It has also taught me that I can conquer the world, meaning that I can do anything and everything my mind and heart desire because I know that I can move by myself and start over anywhere. Second lesson I've learned is that I need to continue to share my story. My father served as my inspiration and growing up, all I ever thought was "If he could move from LA to Atlanta, then I can move across the country too". Not everyone has a mentor/father-figure like mine, so I have chosen to continue to share my story as inspiration for others. I want others to know and understand that they too can do everything I am doing. All it takes is self-inspiration and self-trust, and you can do it! Lastly, the last lesson I've learned is that you can always go back home. Many people are scared to take the leap of faith and to move because they don't want to leave their comfort zone. Well, the truth of the matter is, if you move out, and then you want to move back home, you always can. Give the move a try and if it's not for you, then you can go back! Nothing in this life is permanent.

The move from the south to Seattle has truly shaped me into who I am today. As a college graduate, you think that you have your life mapped out and you are ready to take on the 'real-world.' The truth is that we never really have our life fully figured out and understanding this has helped me live life to the fullest. I continue to love my friends and family more than ever, and I act as if every day is my last. This journey has made me one of the happiest people on this earth due to self-gratification, and I try my best to make someone's day when I see they are down.

Follow my blog: itsmillennialtalk.com
Instagram: @chase_coleman
LinkedIn: linkedin.com/chasecoleman27
Facebook: facebook.com/chasecoleman331

CINDY NOLTE

Today, I am an Amazon best-selling author, a Huffington Post Contributor, a Thrive Global Writer, a TedX Speaker and a TV talk show host but none of my accomplishments were part of my original plan for my future.

Ten years ago I was a young professional who earned a six-figure salary in a career that I enjoyed. I was a regional trainer for a private postsecondary university. I felt like I was making a difference. I enjoyed working with those who reported to me as well as my supervisors. I loved being the go-to person in our region to solve problems. I was passionate about leading my team to new levels-levels that some individuals didn't think they were capable of achieving. Everything was comfortable but I questioned if there was something that I was supposed to be doing that was more meaningful.

I had a growing desire to help people in a more profound way. I had a new passion that I wanted to integrate into my career. I was a student of a variety of holistic modalities for many years and they changed my life. I felt like working in the holistic field would allow me to have a deeper impact on people's lives. I worked about sixty hours a week. I knew that I would not be able to explore my other interests and meet the expectations of my organization. I didn't want to give up my comfortable salary but I also never wanted to look back on my life and wish that I took chances. My husband and his business partner offered me a position in which they would match my salary and allow me time to grow my own business on the side. I crunched numbers of start-up expenses. I reviewed our household budget. I created what appeared to be a very logical plan, but soon I realized that nothing would happen as I expected.

I made the decision to accept the new position that my husband and his business partner offered me so that I could launch my own business on the side. Although I was unsure of exactly where I wanted to take my business, all I knew was that I wanted to change people's lives in a positive way while growing my husband and his business partner's venture in my day job. I excelled in my new position by growing their advertising substantially, however the agreement that they made with me was not honored. Unbeknownst to me, there was tension building behind the scenes. Eventually due to disagreements within their partnership, the business partnership was dissolved. The disharmony and broken promises tainted the new position for me. It did not take me long to realize that it was time for me to walk away from my new position. I was embarrassed, angry, hurt and felt downright betrayed. As I replayed the experience in my mind, I had to acknowledge that there were red flags that I chose to ignore. My gut told me something wasn't right but I wanted to believe otherwise.

I was numb. My safety net was gone. The person that I desperately wanted to turn to for comfort was part of the obstacle that I needed to overcome. My home life and my career were no longer a place of sanctuary for me. As I began to feel again, I felt lonely and defeated. I didn't know where to turn.

I went from thinking that I had everything figured out to feeling like my whole future was uncertain. Through meditation, I connected with my Creator for comfort and direction. I realized that my negative emotions continued to hold me back but it was challenging for me to move through them. I pushed myself to learn from the experience. I was known for being a positive person but for a period of time I lost focus on what I had in my life that was positive. As I continued to search for insight, the lessons began to flow. My first lesson was that my negative emotions allowed the situation to rob me of the joy that I could experience as a result of what I had to be grateful for in other areas of my life. Another lesson was about honoring my inner voice. I knew that I had warning signs not to accept the position with my husband and his business partner but I ignored them. I wanted to believe everything that they told me. I learned to always listen to my gut- even if it doesn't make sense emotionally. I will never let my desire to believe somebody override what my intuition is telling me again. I learned that things don't always happen on my time schedule-fast or slow. Sometimes an incident that appears to be negative may be the very incident that propels me exactly where I am meant to be. My plan was to slowly grow my business. After my ordeal, I was even more motivated to succeed with my own business and jumped in with both feet. It forced me to be focused on my goals for my company. Others may hurt me, but I knew it was up to me how I would allow the experience to affect me. I refused to allow a negative experience to change who I was. Lastly, I learned that sometimes people make promises that they want to believe that they can keep but they really are not capable of following through. I place value on relationships based on all of an individual's actions; not one incident. I forgave my husband for his part in what appeared at the time to derail my career.

I adopted an attitude of peace. Individuals detected the message that I was sending subconsciously. Through my challenging career change people commented on how peaceful I appeared to be all of the time. Unaware of what I had experienced, some of my clients insisted that it was because of my chosen profession that I never appeared to be stressed-as if I didn't have a care in the world. People continued to ask me how I always seemed to be so peaceful for years. Over time it became clear that I needed to write my book, ***Finding Peace in an Out of Control World***, which became an Amazon best-seller. My book led to speaking opportunities and other writing opportunities. Things didn't go as planned but when I let go of what didn't turn out, my future was even better than I planned.

If I hadn't experienced the change in my career as I did, I wouldn't be the person that I am today. I understand that my life is a journey. The experience equipped me with valuable tools that I used on the next step of my journey and that I will continue to use for the rest of my life.

I don't have everything figured out yet, but I know that I am never alone. Everything that I have accomplished is because of God. When I experience a time of uncertainty, I will continue to meditate and seek guidance from above. As long as He is in charge, I know that I am in good hands.

Follow me! https://twitter.com/FreshLookonLife
Like me: https://www.facebook.com/freshlookonlife/
Watch my TED Talk! https://www.youtube.com/
watch?v=sB1RuLNuu7s&feature=youtu.be

Daniel Alegi

RIPE AND RESTART

I've taught myself a motto: "start anywhere", a notion that underscores how the GPS of your life/career/story matters less than where you're actually headed. Direction counts, not status. How far was I willing to go until the winds would blow my way?

I learned to teach film from trying to find my way across story ideas. I love a challenging Sudoku at the crossroads of logic and soul: what will happen next in the puzzle of personal, cinematic storytelling? What are the borders?

My luck gave me a juicy education and three unforgettable mentors. Each invited me (in a different, unique way) into their personal filmmaking process, tools to sculpt my own story with. Resources, intuition and training are the core craft of storytelling.

One day my American dreaming whistled by and I was standing at that train station.

5:00 AM, my writing hour. I just finished a piece about my award-winning 16 mm. film "Czar Of MakeBelieve" (1999), that's before terrorism and stolen elections, before Iphones and climate-change. My 30 minute film, miraculously, had been well received in festivals, even of the Oscar-qualifying kind. I was surprised about the response because it was avant-garde, and not entertaining. My work had turned out as a semi-poetic personal narrative about immigrants with shadows longer than their ambitions, trapped in the bleak landscapes of the American Midwest. My story was metaphor about finding a place to be, an existential dilemma packaged in black and white melancholia, ripe with images of empty buses and sausage factories, Russian mechanics sharing breakfast vodka. And a projectionist, of course. If the Milwaukee River seemed flooding with abandoned chapters of insignificant lives, well it was, and my own journey to the sources of the filmmaking Nile (I was headed for LA) was dripping in machine oil and rusted idealism.

I presented my 5AM piece at a conference in Hattiesburg, MS - on the dry side of New Orleans. I made my classic pitch in favor of cinematic literacy: "the more people know how to make films, the more we will be able to decode an image-based planet." But that day from the podium, folks in ties and jackets were stepping briskly out of the room out towards the Bourbon street city bus tour. By the time my talk was done, there was only one person left in the audience, and I was ready to go back to California, dog and pony and all.

The man was himself thin as a stray hound, bald, bright as a halogen light. He clapped, like in the opening scene of "Little Miss Sunshine", where the hero is a loser motivational speaker in a cold empty space. And that was me… The professor mentions Finland and Hungry. 20 minutes later at dinner he offers me a summer job to teach film-practice in Sweden, where he says he runs a university film department. Why me? He says my film was not American and cinematic, all intended as a compliment. (I had screened the film too) The catch? He was inviting me to nowhere land. To shoot with kids with zero film experience. The pay? Great, including health insurance. I accepted.

I flew back to Santa Monica. Storytelling evenings with my kids and my life-saving soulmate Daniela are my heart's equivalent of extra-glaze doughnuts for Homer Simpson. I told my family crew two stories, the first about a film festival in Italy I screened at before the conference, and then about the Scandinavian job offer. At a festival in Sienna, Italy I screened "Czar" and went into a Q&A. Ask a mechanic about a motor and he will go further with details than the car owner can.

I was asked to leave the stage as a documentary about Iraki children smuggling truck tires over the mountains to Iran on donkeys, was next. The festival director stepped on stage and offered a compromise idea: "We have a room open to anyone who would want to listen to more of Daniel."47 people came to my improve, 2 hour extended Q&A.

The second story was this "I am invited to travel to Finland to work on some films with students".
It was at the time translating the Simpsons for Italian DVD and editing film. The answer I got at home was: I heard it's nice there. Work travels, and film is the language of the world. I had already accepted.

In Finland I was hosted by a local tech-institute, met "my" group of students and an incredible situation: free equipment, props, help and a shooting studio near the town of Jacobstad, where Friday night entertainment is tractor races in the only square with girls sitting on the hoods.

If there is one thing that will change your life, it's making a free two week film without a budget in a place with nothing else going on. Years later, I met Roger Corman, and he told the story of giving young Coppola 3 days to shoot a feature. Awesome. My experience was less memorable perhaps in absolute terms, but a life-changer. We produced one film ("Flower Of Choice") about an old man who revisits his lifetime memories. We invited town folk and their classic cars as extras too. The film had it's a special personal depth, the physical visitation of one's choices, friendships and emotions. Something we do all the time, restarting ourselves with identity.

The next year I returned to make another student film in Finland, a war story based in the Winter War resistance against the Nazis. Old uniforms, no budgets. I wish it to anyone who is in the business to try making movies with young people, freely. This from a maker who had recently moved to Hollywood! What a restart, heading East instead. Mentoring young filmmakers became and still is my vocation. Shortly later, in 2003, I moved my base and my company Cinemahead to Sweden from California, with my family. I have since mentored and co-produced over 3000 short films and lead hundreds of workshops and courses in personal filmmaking and story development. In 2009 I co-founded the YouthCinema organization, based in Tromsoe, Norway to support films by makers under 25 make movies with public funds.

website: www.cinemahead.com
Facebook: @cinemahead / @scriptonite / @docmob / @dannyalegi
Twitter: @danny alegi / @cinemahead / @storychess
Instagram: @cinemaheads
LinkedIn: linkedin.com/in/alegi

DAVID FISHER

I am David, a forty-five-year-old US Army veteran of more than twenty five years. I served in several branches of the army, moving around to address the needs of the army at various times and to adjust to my own developing person and my own changing body. I was an intelligence soldier for the first twelve years. I spent eight as supply and the remainder as transportation. Even with that simplification, I filled many other slots to include a combat engineer spot and an artillery spot over the years.

I have spent many years away from my wife and children, nearly more away from them than I have spent at home when you count all the training time next to all the years in various combat zones. That would be my single greatest regret, but it would be too easy to identify. It is hard to look back at each separate decision point and consider the alternative path that might have occurred, but did not.

About the time I had 15 years invested in the army, I suddenly had a few job offers seemingly "out of the blue." One seemed less solid but was for around $70k/year. A second was a solid offer to do something slightly out of my element, but something that I was capable of doing, for a bit more than my military pay, around $60k/year. At the same time a long term officer friend of mine was interested in starting a business and made the mistake of trusting the wrong people in doing his market research while he was seeking financing. He wanted me as his operations manager, possibly a part-time position as we got the business moving. That business concept rapidly got swallowed up by what is now a very large and successful defense contractor. A former soldier of mine got hired to do things I taught her to do and was hired at the $70k/year rate also. I saw a very nice position with a big contractor go to a very junior airman along with its $150k/yr long-term secure paycheck.

Those are paths, other than retirement, after years of dealing with 9/11 aftermath, I might have selected. But I did not. Most of those jobs could easily have evaporated after just a few years. I chose to finish what I had started, no matter what. It just seemed like a mistake to work through so much hard stuff and quit to do something easy when I was so near to the 20-year mark. I had no idea it would take me another five and a half years past the 20-year mark to finally retire.

While in Iraq, my house was half destroyed by a plumbing break in the downstairs. It flooded the entire downstairs destroying our storage area, two bedrooms, the game room and our library (over 6000 volumes actively collected over 25 years). Insurance refused to cover much of the damage due to little loopholes they found. I lost all my savings, over $45,000 and spent a couple years trying to replace more things. Then, I had a second similar disaster. It was psychologically devastating with no insurance support and the savings already gone.

I was always the leader that took care of his people first, then the people next to him, and the other people nearby, then crashed eventually -somewhere. I used quiet alone activities to recharge myself. I failed, however, to pay the closest attention to the needs, attributes, and developing characteristics of my own children. Interacting with a wife and children became increasingly difficult as I did more and more things in the military. THAT is the one thing I regret most, the reduction of my ability to relate to children and my delayed investment in their development. Children grow older day by day and never stop growing despite our troubles and trials. The day a child is born, we must focus on our child first.

After retirement, I had the initial thought that I would continue doing something related to something I had done in the past, something I was well-qualified and experienced in doing. After experiencing so much destruction in my personal life, I just felt a bit lost as I was going through the interview processes though. No matter how impressed CEOs or hiring managers seemed to be with me, I felt uncomfortable moving into indoor cubicle type jobs, and I did not want to work in transportation taking me away from home all the time.

I discovered a much earlier desire that I had largely forgotten. I love growing plants, and I love animals. I do not mind arduous labor, and I know how to organize things, how to solve problems, and how to serve in many different roles. It is not easy, but I am now back in college studying horticulture, things completely different from my prior degree in psychology and business. While I might not require a degree to work in my chosen field, I need new credentials to help gain financing to fund my new future as an organic herb, fruit and nut grower.

Debbie Salmon

Trusting the Magic of New Beginnings

September 1, 2016 arrived in its uniformed fashion, just as it had for the last twenty-four years. As is customary the girls would proudly wear their pristine dubonnet tunics and gray blouses; and this would be complemented by shiny black shoes and white socks. They would stylishly sling their new backpacks filled with new books over their shoulders. And oh, the smell of new books always made me excited. It was a sweet nervous excitement that was filled with promises of success. There would be new faces too… a couple hundred students and several teachers would be eagerly awaiting an excellent educational experience. The thought of it all energized me. I could not contain my joy, but as I leapt out of bed and skipped to the bathroom reality struck. I looked at ME in the mirror. I heard myself say, "This is a new September morning, one like no other. There are no uniforms, no new books. Certainly, I had a new name and a new agenda. Change had come. Had change chosen me or had I chosen change?" My joyful self knew that either way it did not matter.

Here's how I got here. I had resigned my job as a teacher of English after twenty-four years. Honestly, when I began teaching in September 1992 at one of the top 3 high schools in Jamaica I had no idea that I would remain there for twenty-four years. Within two years of employment I had been promoted to the Senior Staff and within five years I had been assigned at least four different senior positions. I became a young successful educator who had experienced rapid growth and development both at the local and national levels. I was a master of my craft. One illustration of my success was evidenced in my being employed by the Ministry of Education in Jamaica to design the National Curriculum for English Language for Grades 7 – 11 for High Schools in Jamaica. It was a success. At the end of that project I was invited by several schools across the country to facilitate seminars in the teaching and learning of English Language to both teachers and students. Over the years I had received several awards for being an excellent teacher.

High expectations were held of me and the next level of promotion in my teaching career was to become a school principal. Soon I was invited to act as a Vice-Principal at the high school at which I was employed. The opportunity came when the Vice-Principal went on four months' vacation leave. When the acting-period ended I was enlightened. My suspicion that I had no desire to be a school principal was confirmed. During the period most of my energy was spent taking care of my students' social and emotional intelligence rather than their mental abilities. While I was good at it, I hated it. Most days it left me depressed. I loved pedagogy, not guidance and counseling and school principals spent much of their time counseling. Did this mean that I had to leave teaching? I told myself that it didn't; so I kept going. I kept abreast of various new teaching methodologies; I was determined that I would remain relevant, especially in the new dispensation where Computer Technology ruled and the 21st Century teenage learners brought challenges. They didn't learn well from 20th Century teaching styles. Indeed, the age of technology had dawned and while I kept current I felt stagnant. Truthfully, I had plateaued; I had reached the pinnacle of classroom teaching. I was tired of teaching and everything that came with it. I had given all I had to the education system. I had to do something else … but what; teaching was all I had ever done – it was what I knew. I felt trapped and like so many of my colleagues I began to cloak myself in guilt for harboring thoughts of resigning… walking away from everything I had built. Was I crazy? Was I throwing my life away? And then there were my other aspirations – I wanted to make indelible contributions to our family business. Also I had relished dreams of becoming a world renowned author, but these were slowly looking like an impossible feat. I felt that time was slipping away. I drew upon the strength I had shown when I had my first and only child while working in a hostile environment that required unmarried women to resign their jobs if they became pregnant. Yeah, I know it sounds incredible in this twenty-first century! I stood my ground, made a few compromises but refused to resign. I survived that challenge. So I knew I was strong… I could resign. I could walk away. The opportunity to do so came in August 2016 when I married my partner, best-friend and father of my daughter. That meant moving to a different parish, and of course beginning a new job! Now I could also get on with writing… becoming the kind of author I had dreamt of being.

It was "*time to start something new and trust the magic of new beginnings.*" I couldn't wait to start my new job, my new life. It wasn't the usual September, but it was one to remember.

My new workplace was not unfamiliar. After all, I had spent several summers, other holidays plus innumerable weekends there. It was our family business, but the permanence of my presence there loomed large in my mind. So on my first day on the job I hastened to discover my assigned tasks. Filled with warm anticipation I leaned against my partner's office door jam and asked him, "What shall I start doing?"

"Huh? Find something Lady Samson," he drawled my new name with a cursory glance. He believed in my ability to fit in and be directly involved in the business. I was filled with uncertainty and my incredulity was palpable. I thought that because he was my husband he knew that I needed directives. There were no students, no lesson plans, and no whiteboards! This was not school. I stood there awaiting information about the specific tasks he wanted me to do. None came. Eventually, I threw my intelligence around my shoulders and confidently went to my desk and looked for something to do. It was challenging. Embarking on a new beginning isn't always easy I thought as I rummaged through several filing cabinets. Soon I realized that there was much to be done; so I began rearranging my office space. When the day ended I felt accomplished and even more satisfied when my partner indicated his approval. So began several weeks of filing, answering phone calls, completing cash analysis books, making payroll, arranging block deliveries, visiting excavation sites, purchasing heavy equipment and motor vehicle parts. The latter involved traveling to various places. It was different. It was adventurous. It was exciting! My new job did not start with a specific description, truly it was multidimensional. Gradually, my role in our family business became clearer. One precious bonus is that it gave me more control of my time - I could actually focus on writing – the beginning of an additional career!

I am sure that the purse of time given to us offers new opportunities. It is to be spent wisely and we have to trust the magic of new beginnings.

Debbie proudly displaying the Excellent Teacher's Award she received in November, 2015

Debbie (Lady Samson) checking out a D9H Bulldozer at a quarry

DEBBIE ZIMMERMANN

Starting Over –A New Beginning

New beginnings happen every day. For my mom, her journey began when the angels took her to heaven.

It was only a few months ago when I said goodbye to my mom. I am grateful I held her hand as she took her last breathe. I took comfort knowing she was ready for her next chapter. And it was truly an honor to help her transition peacefully from this world.

I thought the toughest part about losing my mom would be saying goodbye but as it turns out, the hardest part is learning to live without her. I try to fill the void and the emptiness inside my heart every day.

I had a mother who loved me completely. I realize how precious it is to have loved someone so much that it hurts when they leave.

I believe my mom's spirit and our memories together will live on forever. These are gifts that can never be taken away. I continue to appreciate how many ways my mom impacted my life and how she prepared me for my new beginning....living my life without her.

This new beginning feels like an ending because letting go is hard. I'm fighting to hold onto the way things were. The easy days are easy and the challenging days are testing me to my core. I'm learning to focus on the joy in my life. I need to embrace this change rather than fight it. I know I don't have to have it all figured out to move forward. I try and remember the tiniest step forward is progress.

I'm learning to embrace where I am in this journey. I know it's not easy but I believe the best is yet to come. I've taken a look at what's constant in my life hoping this foundation will give me the strength and courage to move forward.

Memories of my mom will live on. The holidays, birthdays, and all our special moments together are cherished in my heart. As the days go on, I will continue to laugh, smile, cry, and ask myself why my mom was taken away from me.

I will learn to accept my feelings, and appreciate that each day is a building block for the next one.

DEBORAH STANSIL

Officially, my story began in February 2015, although you could say it actually started in the early nineties when I was at primary school. It was then that I discovered a love for creative writing.

Of course, at ten years old, it wasn't a life changing experience. There was no light bulb moment. It was just something I enjoyed doing – writing stories. Life continued as expected and once I left school, the writing stopped, over taken by real life commitments.

There was always this idea in the back of my head that one day I'd write a novel, but it was always just a pipe dream – something I would say I was going to do, but never really thought I would do. Even when I talked about doing it, I never really expected to actually do it.

Then in February 2015, something changed. I don't know what exactly, but I decided it was time to write. I didn't know where to start, and having not written anything for almost seventeen years, a novel seemed big. Too big. So I started a blog.

I remember sitting there, my laptop open on my knee. And this idea just hit me that I should start a blog. I had no idea how to do that, what I would write about or what it entailed. I Googled blogging, and the first hit was for Blogger. It seemed simple enough, and away I went.

I happily wrote my first blog post and within days it had me. I well and truly had the writing bug again. A couple of months later, I bought my own domain and went self-hosted on my blog. That's when I knew I was serious about writing.

Before too long, I started working on my first novel. My novel was released in 2016, but I still wanted more. I enjoyed writing in my spare time, but it wasn't enough. I started to feel like my job was holding me back. I felt like I was cheating myself when I went to work – I shouldn't be there; I should be writing.

I began looking into the possibility of freelance writing, hoping that one day I would be able to cut my working hours down to part time and make enough to top up my income from freelancing. Before I knew it, I was ghost writing other people's novels and stories and writing articles. And being paid for it.

My goal was to leave my full time job and to be writing for a living by the end of 2017. I wasn't sure if that was a realistic possibility or not, but I knew I had to aim for it.

October of 2016 rolled around and something told me that if I didn't do this now, if I didn't leave my day job and write full time, I never would. A little voice in my head knew it was the right time for me.

I was in the pub where I worked when this epiphany hit me and it hit me like a brick wall. Luckily, it was a Tuesday afternoon so it was pretty quiet. I got a piece of paper and a pen and I worked out my monthly expenses and whether or not I realistically thought I could cover them from writing alone.

I was eighty percent sure I could, and I told myself I should wait until I was certain, but that voice was getting louder and I couldn't ignore it. And just like that, I made the decision that changed my life. I wrote my resignation letter that night and handed it in the next morning.

I had no safety net, no B plan. Just a love for writing and the determination to make it in a world that I loved. That was six months ago. And I'm still making a living as a full time writer. Something I had never even considered was a possibility for a normal girl like me.

I'm still convinced that if I had have waited, I would never have had the courage to leave a secure, full time position for a job riddled with rejection and uncertainty. I am also still convinced that this is the life for me, and if I hadn't have taken the chance when I did, I would forever regret it.

I took my chance and I went for it. I now have two novels and two short story collections published. I have another short story collection on the horizon, two more novels to be written this year and two non-fiction books too. I am still blogging and ghost writing as well.

I am constantly busy, my mind constantly whirring with ideas – and I love it. To think how close I came to spending the rest of my life working for someone else and pushing my own dreams aside scares me.

If you are offered the chance to live your dream, take it – because if you don't, someone else will.

Bio:

Deborah A Stansil is a thirty something writer living in the North East of England. She has a love for all things writing and reading related and if she isn't writing, you will most often find her reading a novel with a coffee (or glass of wine) or procrastinating on social media!

To keep up to date with Deborah, visit her blog, My Random Musings or follow her on Twitter (where she spends far too much of her time!)

www.myrandommusings.co.uk
Twitter   @randommusings29

Diana Matthews

A Canadian in Brooklyn

The most exciting, challenging, and significant relationship of all is the one you have with yourself. - Carrie Bradshaw

Last summer, I changed my life.

I was (and still am) working for a feminist film distribution company and in May 2016, we launched our first feature-length film called *Dream, Girl*, a documentary showcasing the stories of inspiring and ambitious female entrepreneurs.

We screened the film at the White House, hosted our sold-out premiere in NYC, booked screenings as near as Westchester, New York and as far as Auckland, New Zealand and put in place our sales team to facilitate the growth of this powerhouse movement.

I also decided to move to New York City.

It was a decision that felt like it had been years in the making. A lifetime, really. It had been burbling below the surface, waiting for the right time to manifest itself as an opportunity, rather than a dream.

It's just so strange when that transition actually happens.

I had moved away from home four years ago to attend grad school in Ottawa. The pace of the program was intense and the work was relentless. It didn't take long before my yoga routine and (somewhat) balanced diet that I had established in my undergraduate studies took a back-seat to projects, deadlines, and chasing leads.

The value in setting aside a few hours a week to dedicate to my practice quickly diminished as I immersed myself in the demands of the degree.

It took a toll. And I knew that when Erin Bagwell and Komal Minhas, the co-founders of *Dream, Girl*, asked me to move to New York City, I would have to make taking care of my emotional and mental well-being a priority.

One of the things I felt so grateful for during the move was the incredible community I entered into. The generosity and inclusivity I've already experienced in the city has given me immeasurable peace of mind. The amount of like-minded people I met throughout the process showed me I am where I belong.

I am where I belong.

It feels surreal to type, let alone say out loud.

Being a pop culture junkie from as early as I can remember, much of my viewing, listening and cultural experience has been defined by New York. This is not unique. The saturation and dominance of film, television, fine art, and music out of the Big Apple is what has made it one of the most influential cities in the world.

I've been in love with NYC since Rachel Green walked out of the rain and into Central Park wearing her sopping wet wedding dress.

That love was reinforced as I watched Carrie Bradshaw and her three best friends shop and sip their way around Manhattan, one Manolo Blahnik, and cocktail at a time.

And the soundtracks to Rent and Wicked provided the background music to all three years of my high school experience (which was ideal because Broadway is the only genre that could keep up to that kind of drama!)

To me, these aren't clichés. They're the characters and spaces I saw myself reflected in as I developed my own identity and sense of media literacy.

I've been told for most of my life that pop culture is shallow, meaningless, and a complete waste of time.

When my biggest dream was to become a MuchMusic VJ and interview celebrities on the red carpet, my best friends were thinking of going into accounting, medical school, and engineering.

It's not that there's anything wrong with those professions, it just made me feel like my interests lacked value. I even struggled to find friends who shared my passion for feminism.

I've been lucky in that my interests have always been rooted in visual media. Whether it's TV or filmmaking, storytelling through imagery and sound is what gets me going. When I found *Dream, Girl* and connected with Erin and Komal, my interests were no longer fringe, silly, or unattainable. They were within my reach and infused with meaning - a meaning that had worth.

I've spent the past year working alongside women that have become my family. I'm no longer worried that I should've taken a different path or that my dreams aren't enough. Sure, the vision has changed somewhat, but to be honest - not by much.

With so much going on in this post-launch phase, the *Dream, Girl* office is a busy hive of activity, an absolutely wonderful feeling. But I know that in order to be my best self on this team, there are certain aspects needed to take care of in the transition process.

I've often felt a need to "go it alone." I fiercely value my independence, almost to a point of dysfunctional martyrdom. In archetypal language, this is often identified as the Orphan Child, a character who feels that they must achieve success and go through life alone in order for it to be valuable.

I'm an external processor and after living in New York for almost a year, I've learned that taking care of myself isn't just a nice thing to do - it's absolutely mandatory. And a big part of that self-care is letting others in on my experience.

The pace of our work, the demands of the city, and the adjustment of living on the other side of the continent from my family has forced me to embrace change and find comfort in the discomfort. Leaning on my team, my friends, and the extended network I've connected to have pulled me through tough days and uplifted me on the good ones.

Although this move marked a new chapter in my life, it didn't feel as though I was starting over. It felt more like a continuation and profound validation of my identity, as if a path that was all my own was just inviting me to take the first step.

After finding an apartment in Brooklyn last June, I met up with a group of friends and watched the Tony Awards Red Carpet at the Beacon Theatre. As the cameras flashed and an endless parade of genetically blessed superstars waved at loyal onlookers, I couldn't help but smile. It was the perfect activity to take part in after making the decision to be there.

A couple of weeks later, I watched Sarah Jessica Parker work the shoe department at Bloomingdale's as promotion for her brand.

My passion for empowering women is only amplified by my love of culture. Being my best self in NYC and stepping into this new adventure is something I'm still figuring out. To know that the work I'm a part of is striving to facilitate the growth of female storytelling and encourage women to find their voice is incredibly humbling.

To feel seen and supported in a city of 8 million people is something that I do not take for granted.

This is what I love. And I no longer need to apologize for it.

DON WARREN

It was a fall day in 2001 when I looked in the mirror and said, "What the hell are you doing here? You don't want to wear that suit." 9/11 had made me question where my path was leading to, seeing how life can change in an instant. I knew I had a calling; to do something I felt was meaningful, and working as a spoke in a large company wheel was not it. I wanted...needed to start over. I had always wanted to impact lives, as my father did through his counseling, which I admired so deeply.

I left that job shortly after my divorce and had very little to live on. As long as I made certain my ex-wife and children were set, I could take the time to focus on building a career that satiated my inner calling and, in turn, be happier, making myself a better person and father for my sons.

A few years prior, I had been working on a design for an electric guitar that was unlike any before it. It wound up securing an endorsement deal with Arlen Roth (Nashville Session Legend), whom I admired so greatly. I was making a handful of these guitars for people around the country and was regarded as a top-notch luthier among those in a small, niche community. However, I was not getting the national recognition I needed to make it a full-time living. I was feeling discouraged, barely scraping by. There even came a time when I had to live in my car for a couple of weeks. Rock-bottom was where I was and rock-bottom was where I knew I would spring from. I am (to put it into football terms) a "4th – and - long with 5 seconds on the clock" player. A calm had come over me. The pressure was nothing more than a thought, and I knew I would prevail. It's just the way I was, and with that, I went to a local music school that needed a guitar teacher. I spoke with Ed Munger, the gentleman who ran the program. We talked, and after a few minutes, he simply said "it's yours." I will never forget those words. My life was completely changed. Of course, I was nervous. Sure, I could play guitar - but could I compare to teachers with years of training and experience? I knew this would be an enormous challenge. I also knew I would have to study harder, project more positivity, and offer my best consistently in order to earn the right to be considered an equal from those I worked with.

Over the next few years, it had become clear to me that this was indeed my calling. Through word-of mouth, I had built a solid reputation, and with that, enough students to venture out on an idea my good friend, Victoria, had suggested. Why not offer a weekend music camp for my students? It started at a local recording studio with a handful of teens jamming on some simple songs, and by end of the weekend (after having rehearsed with one-another), the camp-attendees would perform the tunes for their parents when they would arrive to pick their kids up.

One day, the sister of one of my students came in to watch a lesson. She was very shy and said very little. Something told me to engage her in conversation. Her name was Emily Costa, and during our conversation, she revealed to me that she could sing. A short time later, she started taking lessons and had written her first song. With her new-found confidence, she decided she wanted to attend my music camp. Even though at that time the camp was predominantly attended by male students playing heavier rock tunes, she played her guitar and sang her original pop and alternative-rock songs for the audience at our camp performance and wowed everyone.

Emily's singing and performing eventually lead her to write more songs. Before long, she had inspired many of my teenage students to do the same. No longer the shy little girl, Emily auditioned and landed various roles in her high school's musicals. In the years that followed, she had become the star of her High School plays. Even though she is now a 21-year-old woman living in New York City, she is still the talk of her High School. Emily has developed into a confident and strong young woman. I could not be more proud. Emily has since recorded a CD of original music soon to be released.

Riley Snyder, a 12-year-old, came to me for lessons about the same time as Emily. He enjoyed my teaching method and ended up being my student until he left for Berklee College of Music in Boston. Riley had admired my guitar-making skills, and according to him, my bad "dad" type of humor. Riley would remain my student until he left for school. Due to his parents' salary, he did not qualify for financial assistance, so the two of us decided he would advance so far that he would test out of some classes, with his knowledge exceeding their curriculums. At his audition, he impressed the panel, and was awarded a spot in a highly sought-after class. Not only did he ace the class, he completed his studies in three years and is now teaching guitar with recommendations from Berklee staff and is repairing instruments as well. Seeing the influence I have had on his life is heart-warming.

These are but two stories among many others. The "bigger picture" in all of this, is the way my approach and ability to relate to my students has made an impact on those of all ages. One student, a counselor, informed me that he considers me to be a "music empath." He likes that I am able to relate to my students from a place of understanding, and relating to the position they are at within the learning process.

I am well-aware and blessed that my students look to me as much more than a music instructor. They, and their parents, have often remarked that they feel I am a positive role model and mentor for their kids. In everything I do, I seek to impart a sense of empowerment and overall confidence that is missing from many people's lives. My camps teach kids and teens how to approach a difficult task and apply themselves as well as to develop clear, concise communication skills in order to reach their goals in a short time frame. They learn when and how to take the lead, when to follow, and how to stand strong when it feels like it just isn't coming together.

What is the one thing I am the most proud of? To this day, I get comments from professionals who were once students of mine telling me that my approach has helped them not only be better in their work lives, but better at communicating with their children. I started over by changing my own life to open the possibility for me to impact lives just as my father did. I have worked hard to make a modest living and am often called "the best kept secret" in my area. It saddens me when I observe people giving up on their musical dreams and goals because they were not working with someone that could inspire them to be so much more.

Today, my son Mike also teaches at Drome Sound. I know he has the ability to take it beyond my wildest dreams. I am passionate about what I do and it kills me to think there is one person out there that will miss a life-changing opportunity simply because they may never come to know what we offer. But... what I can do is continue to make the difference for those we do meet. For that I am thankful.

E-mail: donwlessons@gmail.com
Website: www.donwarrenmusic.com
Facebook: www.facebook.com/donwarrenmusic
Instagram: donwarrenmusic

DONNA PAUL

Steadfast

I spit on my mother. Slobbered right on her face on purpose. I needed to see her spirit afire. Even when I bent close, her gaze remained contemplative. I aimed another bit at her cheek. I smeared the spittle, rubbed it in. She never even flinched.

Though this wasn't one of them, there was a time I blamed her for the aches inside me. Our clan had shattered; my father chose another whole family, bought them a farm, and sold our cottage at the lake. He left me, not us. Disillusioned and broken, my one-time PTA president mother found herself ill-equipped to deal with bills, errands and shopping with no car, and a miserable child. None of our former luxuries remained. We had little happiness and even less hope.

I yearned to witness her resolve as she'd trudged on through our sad little life. I missed her soft hand pulling mine, leaning her shoulder into the hard times. I thought about those times when gossip swirled and she led with her chin set in strong determination.

On the rare occasion she shared a cup of tea with a commiserating friend, I bristled with indignation. We had no money for entertaining – or for extra groceries! Humming without a care in the world, she sliced bread into thin horizontal halves. A light smear of mayonnaise, slices of cucumber so skinny you could read the paper through them, and a sprinkle of salt and pepper followed in careful layers. Her sharp knife flashed as it cut off the crusts and divided each sandwich into four neat triangles. A humiliating pile of twelve scrawny wedges from three pieces of bread! She made me pull out pretty luncheon plates for the round table draped with antique lace. She laughed with her friend until she snorted catching her breath. I slid low in my chair. My friends' mothers were far too refined to carry on like that.

I didn't like that she seemed so jovial. Did she even know that I was wallowing in the confusion of Junior High, hating my protruding tummy? Did she care that every girl in the world but hers had gotten her period? I resented every minute of her happiness. In the years that followed, I came to realize the responsible tenacity it took to recreate both our lives.

...

Armed with fresh saliva I persisted, aiming at her neckline, shoulders and slender arms. At last, she drew herself up, holding her breath. I settled back. Turquoise-blue eyes flashed bright. Her lips pursed in a rosy cupid's bow, a tiny smile somehow tugging at its edges. Although she remained mute, I swear I heard her signature laugh with a couple of good snorts in the middle.

I am not a conservator, but I followed a centuries-old restoration method for cleaning oil paintings. Cotton swabs and plain ole spit work wonders to bring aged canvases back to sharp and warm. As though wet, brush strokes crisscross facial features, the ruffles of a silk blouse and a gleaming silver pin. Ridges and valleys of paint coax that special glow of a woman in her late thirties, blissful and unaware of her future. I fit my mother's portrait back into its pine frame and hung it in her rightful place. A porcelain urn with ashes and her tea set wait on the piano below.

EILEEN DOYON

Starting over………..I have started over so many times in my life…I lost count. Some by my choice and others not, but I have always grown and learned something. After my Dad died in 2011, my next plan was gloomy and dark, then my book series came to life in 2013 and that gave me life again. It carried me til 2014 when we started looking at homes back where I grew up, Fort Edward, New York, small town USA. I was looking to start again where all familiar faces and hearts were for me after losing my family throughout the years. We had just come back from an awesome wedding in Fort Edward, and I received a voice mail message that stated, I was laid off. The new owner of the business said that she could not tell me to my face, but I could go to unemployment the next day. She had no money to give me any severance due to business being so bad. I had worked there over 20 years. Well, she had beat me to the punch. I had planned on being the one to quit. It just moved forward our relocating plans. Two weeks later, I slipped shoveling and broke my wrist quite badly. As the doctor said, you did it good, with a metal plate and three screws and, yes, my right hand! I would need a doctor's note for flying from here on in! Who would hire me with a broken wrist and major PT ahead?

The next year was a learning experience. I did get a job working from home twenty five hours a week and was hired without meeting the company. All done thru networking and referrals. I was working on my books, my social media, and loved working from home, however, without medical insurance and a regular pay check, it was another new start for sure. I never had been without cash of my own. Moving forward to the next year/2016, I was searching for a job in New York as well as New Hampshire.

I never wanted to move to New York without a job, previously, and now I found myself with no job and looking to move to New York. The saying goes….follow your heart….it was challenging for me while I had my job to make the move previously. My job had given me cash in my pocket and a lot of flexibility, the golden handcuff syndrome.

I landed a job in New York and my start date was 12/1/16. My cousin in New York had one of his apartments available 12/1/16 and said that I could have it. It was five minutes from where I would be working. Everything was falling into place. We planned on Danny moving out 4/1/17. Danny's mom had bone cancer and it was a horrible experience for him and his family. I kept tossing back and forth about the move and Danny wanted me to go. We were converting his workshop into an apartment and all plans were thrown upside down with his mom's illness.

The news to my friends in New Hampshire and New York was out, and I was going home......how I loved saying those words. This book took on a whole new meaning for me, and I was going for it. Business friends and more importantly, my New York personal friends were all so welcoming and telling me if I needed anything, they were there, and welcomed me with open arms. The week after Thanksgiving, we borrowed my friend's vehicle, and packed up my things bare bones style, air mattress and all. My plan was to come home every weekend to see Danny and my little Ottie (my cat). We got there Thursday and Timmy met us there. It was a cute little apartment and just the right size. Even after no heat for the first two nights, it was going to be perfect!

We met up with friends Saturday night and had a blast. We planned Christmas parties and get togethers....I was in seventh Heaven, and I was home. How I loved to say those words. We got up early Sunday morning and Danny left quickly. We did not want sad goodbyes and knew it would be challenging but things were falling into place. Sunday, I went grocery shopping and walked around town. Danny was going to be dealing with his mom and the apartment by himself. Danny's ride back to New Hampshire was not fun for him. I think reality settled in, and he called. We talked and talked. I felt awful and my heart was not in a good place. I remember the feeling I had when my Dad was dying, and I had Danny as my rock, and I was not alone. How could I do that to him now after all of his support to me? After hours on the phone and many tears, I told him to come and get me on Monday, and I would come back to New Hampshire. We would get through this together and figure things out. You see, when I found out my dad had cancer and a short time to live, I did not move back home. I drove to New York just about every weekend, however, I never forgave myself for not quitting my job and moving home to care for him 24/7. How could I do it to Danny in handling his family situation? Danny drove out on Tuesday, and we packed up and moved me back to New Hampshire.........So my red shoes took me home for five nights and six days.....

I started temping, and Danny was working on our apartment unit, and his mom was getting worse. She died Christmas Eve. 2017 rolled in, The Patriots won The Superbowl with setting all kinds of records, I found a job that I love, and Danny completed the apartment unit. We rented that out 4/1/2017, and things financially settled down. I started this book in January/2017 and was busy working on that with an August 1st release date.

So starting over….a new beginning………well my plans did not work out the way I expected to start over in 2016, but what does starting over really mean……starting again….starting to follow your heart…..but I am following my heart…where will my red shoes land…….for you see…….that is me on the cover of this book. I am wearing my Dad's hat and his trench coat and following the tracks in Fort Edward, New York where we use to party and hang out………..which track do I take………. find out in my next book…….

ELAINE RAU

A year out of college my roommate gave me the nickname "the job collector" because I had worked for so many companies and had held so many positions and titles. I usually worked about two to three jobs at once before I would move on from one and go to another. Even though people told me it wasn't a good idea to job hop so often, I just didn't know what I wanted to do and each job taught me something different about what I was looking for.

I started to see a trend in the jobs I liked which were all somehow related to events, fashion, blogging, and the wedding industry. I finally settled on one job as a wedding sales representative for a large photo and video company in Chicago. I loved working there and once I passed the 3-month mark, I knew I had found a keeper! I started focusing all my energy on that company and rose through the ranks swiftly. In two short years I had become the National Wedding Sales Manager and went from making 20K to 72K a year.

My job was my life and I loved it because I loved what I did. I worked 24 hours a day 7 days a week, I always had my phone on me and took calls at all hours… and was completely oblivious to how my work environment was slowly changing how I viewed myself and my capabilities. I have always considered myself a strong and independent woman, however the longer I was with the company, the less I felt I had to offer to the world and thought that this job was it for me.

It got so bad that I was scared to leave because I didn't think I would find anything better. I didn't realize that this was due to being talked down to every day and having my suggestions devalued at every turn. I am a very creative person so to be locked in a box without flexibility was very hard and what made it worse was that I didn't even know I was being verbally manipulated and abused. It came to a point where I had to get a lawyer to help me quit because my boss wouldn't let me go and I couldn't stand up to him by myself.

After I was finally freed from my ordeal, I cried for a good few days. I was so relieved and at the same time so shocked at myself for letting something like this happen! If it were anyone else I would have called it out a long time ago, but I was blinded by my obsession with my job. My job had become my identity and letting it go wasn't easy. I felt like I had just gone through a messy breakup and my emotions were everywhere, so I decided to just relax for a while. I had so much saved up that I just partied every night and took fun trips with friends. Then after I got that out of my system, I decided to move to Honduras to finally be reunited with my fiancé!

After I moved, things started getting hard again. I was in a completely foreign environment and didn't speak the language either. I felt lonely and purposeless and not being able to find a job that I enjoyed didn't help either. Once again I was fully reliant on a man, my fiancé, and I hated it. Luckily he is the most patient, kindhearted, and compassionate man in the world and was able to see past my hurtful words and angry episodes and walk beside me towards healing my hardened heart. He spoke highly of me and encouraged me every single day to not worry about anything else except finding my own path.

I decided to figure out what my biggest motivations in life were so I could get my life back on track. By looking deep into the core of my being, I realized that I had a passion to elevate women in business and that I have always wanted to be in business for myself, but just didn't know how to do it. I wanted to learn from other ladies to see how they did it and glean knowledge from their insight; however, I couldn't afford a mentor, so I decided to create an interview platform where I could ask them hard questions and learn from their answers.

I drafted a quick idea of what I wanted to do in my head, checked to make sure I was able to use the same name across all social media platforms, then bought my domain (http://www.ladybossblogger.com) and started learning about WordPress and setting my site up. A week later however, I started to lose steam and wanted to quit and go back to what I knew and potentially blog about the wedding industry. But I forced myself to focus and took a chance instead to see if I could monetize it, knowing that would be the driving factor I needed to keep going… and it worked! A few days later I made my first $5 and was ELATED and from that day on my entrepreneurial journey began.

I decided to interview myself on my own blog since I had become an entrepreneur and how I learned how to make money from nothing, you can read it here: www.ladybossblogger.com. Now 9 months later, I look back at all I have accomplished in business and in life, and cannot be more thankful. If I hadn't pulled myself out of my comfort zone and gone into the great unknown, I would not be where I am today. Through this experience, I discovered how much strength I had within and once I started piecing myself back together again, I became a better and stronger version of who I was.

I want to encourage you today and let you know that there is strength inside of you that you may not have discovered yet. A strength that will get you through hard times… a strength that you need to uncover.

FOLLOW US
Facebook @ladybossblogger
Instagram @ladybossblogger
Twitter @ladybossblogger
Pinterest @ladybossblogger
Website www.ladybossblogger.com
Reviews www.ladybossblogger.com/testimonials
Reviews www.facebook.com/pg/ladybossblogger/reviews

ELIZABETH GARRISON

Approximately two years ago, I was awakened by a police call at 1:35am. On February 24, 2015. The moment that changed my life forever. One of the most dreaded, undesirable nightmare a mother would want to dream of. This was a reality, a heartbreaking, heart wrenching labor of the heart. My daughter, Candace Elizabeth had died by the hands of her beloved husband. It took me two years to wake up and realize after her death that I needed to make a decision, am I going to sit here and die a little more each day, or take baby steps and live again?

I lost everything. I lost my first born daughter, Candace Elizabeth, my career, my car, my home, and I lost me. Who Am I? I am the mother of an angel in heaven now. I bought a new car and paid it off. I moved back to my home where I grew up with my parents, who are now in heaven too. I decided that I am starting over at the age of 55. I settled in my home, taking care of my Aunt who is 92, rearing my youngest daughter, Sierra, who is 14 and in high school this year, along with my grandson, Jaden, who has Cystic Fibrosis, whom I am adopting, and my oldest grandson, Skyler, who is 14, and continues to, and still struggles with the death of his mom, my daughter.

I am in college at Paul Mitchell, the school in North Carolina. I am a Certified Makeup Artist and still attending as a Future Professional with Paul Mitchell with GPA of 98.08. It has been the most rewarding choice I have made for me. I plan to graduate in November of 2017 and work with theatre and open my own salon. I have children depending on me that I love and treasure.

My daughter, Candace, is with me in my heart everywhere I go. I breathe for her and live for her children so she can love them through me. Every day is a new day, and I am always just a breath away to being with her again.

My life story is not over. This is a new start…….a new beginning.

ELIZABETH JOYCE

Just Dog

A home and a heart broken wide open.

When asked …. What made you decide to "start over" … What came to mind was … what do you mean … Isn't that what everybody does … but then it got "personal" … no Libby, If you could recall a particular moment in your life that caused you to go in a completely new direction with new hopes and new dreams and embracing the unknown and you ended up "starting over" with firm footing forward … My only response and indeed a validated answer is just this …. It was common sense, logic, and reasoning with an honest outlook into a home and heart that was broken wide open, but I knew I had good intentions for the greater good … And that's the moment I realized I needed to write this story! Feelings mattered, then, and now … But the difference between feelings and integrity and the only thing that stands in the way from doing what's right anyways even when it's hard … Is ones' pride and ego … That's the key to unlocking any door to change your own destiny … In that one paragraph. But it wasn't easy in the beginning. But! Only in the beginning!

There was not anything that happened to me that hasn't happened to many other people the same way (or worse). We just don't talk about it. I do not think I'm anyone better to have had integrity for the greater good. I chose what was best for my child at the time of hearing that his father was expecting another baby with a new life and a new wife; while I could not have any more children, medically. I just did not allow my feelings to cloud my judgment for making choices of what is best for my son. If I could share that knowledge, then I know I've serviced this question well. My point is, in as much to say, that no one is any better or worse off under any circumstances than anyone else. We are all human, and life is good or bad. It all depends on your attitude, your own state of mind, and the wellness from within. I no sooner realized … In the beginning … I wasn't well! There are no two people the same. We are all "different". If I could share one thing, I would share that I learned very quickly that we can experience similar emotions with very different circumstances. I'd like to let others know that they are not alone! Even if and when you feel you are … look up, look out, and look all around. Do not close into yourself ... honestly the worst thing you can do is to go into your head and close into yourself in your own home .... I would recommend through living proof that rather than focus on a bad situation gone worse when I felt alone, I got a dog. I didn't jump into a relationship. I focused on reinventing myself and loving myself for me. I was feeling completely worthless as I has no purpose. I left my job (with no job to replace it with). I knew my feelings were overwhelming me all of the time, and I sought professional help and guidance. I kept being told that everything was my fault, but yet something in me just wanted to fix me ... I knew that it only makes sense that it takes two people working together to make or break a home. After a broken home and a broken heart wide open, I felt that I was a complete failure to my son. The wise choice for my son for moving forward was being able to make the right choice. I could focus on him, and that was providing him with solid opportunities for a bright future. Then I got a dog, that's it. Just a dog ...then I learned how to train him ... and I got good at it ... and I noticed through my own healing over time that other people loved my dog just as much I did. I could take him everywhere I went and others asked me how I trained him and one thing led to another .... and another! Then from there, I changed my career three times, and I followed my passions like the Four Canadian seasons. My only hope is that I am a loving, caring, giving, respectable human being, and a leading role model for my son. This may help others grow to know the same joy and beautiful things about life.

We all have natural born talents and gifts. We all have strengths and weaknesses. If only we could focus on using our own strengths as assets while working on developing our weaknesses into likes for the simple reason of knowing what love is from the inside out. Because in the end, all you need is love, the rest really will just fall into place. I've had a career path change three times and it brought a field of hopes and dreams, an honest heart, and an open mind. I am at peace with myself and confident about all my choices along the way. I was able to embrace all of me, and understand myself. I can honestly be proud of myself and answer to my child or grandchildren of who, what, where, when, and why I did and said what I did throughout my entire life. The choices I did make at any point, I can confidently say and firmly know that those who loved me would never leave me or abandon me (that goes for family, friends, or lovers). It's nothing I would ever take personally ever again! I have nothing but great stories to tell about my embraced life ever since that day I found my home and my heart broken wide open with nothing left except JD "just dog". It is nothing I would go around the country and sing about, but I have indeed enjoyed the journey. Love (from within a right true place in your heart) is all you need and the rest really does just fall into place.

That was his name "JD" just dog .... And it was the first Christmas I had to spend alone knowing my heart was as empty as was my home. I was tipping the scale at nearly 300 pounds. I had a very hard time finding my purpose. I suppose they call that the empty nest syndrome.

This was two years later, and I woke up, and what came to mind after a peaceful sleep was that dog spelt backwards was God. I knew I had to share him with others. So I started volunteering (after passing the test with citizen advocacy) I was able to keep busy with my heart and mind occupied taking me and just dog into nursing homes, hospitals, and in-care patient facilities. There I would teach others and share that therapeutic remedies, stroking and loving a dog, can bring others to a well-state of mind through pet therapy. I was so grateful for my peace of mind and unchanged, honest, and loving kind heart. I had seen so many others conflicted with bitterness from a broken home. I promised myself … I'd never be bitter for as long as I live. Even if I spend my entire life up till my dying days alone, I'll never grow a bitter heart. As time went on even as years went on, JD did eventually pass away. I've remained loyal to the cause. I eventually was able to work with dogs helping to rehabilitate them at a rescue facility. The facility was for aggressive dogs unable to be put back up for adoption and who were listed to be untrained. We learned the techniques of Cesar Milan and had a pack of twenty seven dogs. We worked together as a team at top-dog pet services. We stayed with these dogs around the clock, 24/7, as a pack with human contact and in a pack setting … We had a 98% success rate in rehabilitation with every dog that came in from the nonprofit organization. I've since moved on to training dogs to working with special needs kids. I now volunteer for an organization closer to my heart following in the footsteps of my own mother … With Dreams Take Flight.

ELLA DE JONG

Smiling …

Who would have thought! Was I really 'running away' from it? Running away from 30 years of teaching? The answer is: "yes I was running away, running far from it!" Didn't I have other options? Leaving this class and become a teacher in another class for example. No, sorry, I've been hurt too much in this school. Leaving this school and become a teacher in another school? That should do the trick, one would think. But, again: "No, sorry." I've been in search for my confidence for too long.

I didn't recognize myself anymore while standing in front of a class. Well, some bits and pieces of me as an enthusiastic, creative teacher were still there, but those last two years had almost crushed me. I had to follow the rules "they" thought were best. My intuition told me otherwise, but I listened and I tried. It made me become an uncertain person. I kept on smiling while at school, I kept on working hard for the kids in class, for their parents, for the school in general but boy how crushed I felt!

My colleagues thought it was all due to my divorce. Well, what I think is, hadn't I been divorced and living in my own lovely little old house, for sure I'd become ill for months and/or killed someone while I was throwing stones at school windows. Honestly, if only they knew!

So, as to keep myself out of jail and regain some kind of confidence, I had no other choice than to leave my dearly beloved job and not going back for more than a year!

My income dropped drastically while I threw my heart and soul into my tiny, tiny entrepreneurship. My daughters suddenly had to live with a mum who didn't want to go shopping. Not for clothes, not for food. A mum who didn't want to go to the movies, visit theater, and dine in restaurants any more. My daughters survived and found another mum (kidding). I was 24/7 busy writing, a little coaching, developing a training course, and next to that also being busy with some more writing, some more developing, more coaching and some traveling. This felt so good! I got good reviews and feedback even when I expressed my ideas about teaching and helping troubled kids at school. Who would have thought?

After 18 months I came back as a substitute. Every week is different, every day is different. For two days a week I am now working in an unknown class at an unknown school. I love it! I don't care at what moment they tell me which class and school is expecting me. A week in advance, three weeks in advance, or the very morning at 07:00 o'clock, it really doesn't matter to me! I didn't expect to enjoy my substitute role so much. I love the fact that it's about keeping a close eye on all of the kids and making sure the atmosphere is a friendly one. The most wonderful thing of all is: I'm in charge of HOW we are going to achieve this. I'm the one who sets the rules, who smiles at the misbehaving child, who allows the children to have their five minutes 'free time' even before half an hour has passed! It's because of these rules, we were able to say 'goodbye' with a smile, up to now all 480 of us!

It's unbelievable but true, a few months before my come back, I was a galaxy far away from this smiling feeling. I had failed! In a completely different setting, I had failed again. I was told: "Doing your best is not good enough, Ella". Gosh it hurt so much! I had put my heart and soul in it, I sincerely believed in it! But there I was: a (slightly over) middle aged woman, brave enough to make a new beginning, but still hugely weak enough to let herself be pulled down the drain again! Hadn't I gained some self confidence after almost twelve months doing what I loved? Obviously not … Or was it because of the total surprise? I'm still not sure. We had been preparing this together but when it came down to 'showing our skills', I didn't fit in. My rules were the wrong rules, not good enough … My smiling was misplaced, my 'keeping a close eye on everyone' was probably too much a mummy thing and 'free time', well what I did wasn't okay …

I was devastated, in shock and very emotional the following days. I made some silly mistakes. Have you ever noticed? When you are very uncertain you say the wrong words, you are acting 'weird' while all you really want to do is disappear. It was horrible! How was I going to pick myself up? How was I going to trust myself of being able to teach? Teaching from my heart added with humor and creativity? While crushing my brains and crying my eyes out one night, I looked at the sky. I felt so alone. Suddenly I smiled a little and thought: I need Mother Theresa. She will comfort me, she wouldn't judge anyone. That's what I needed! I sighed and while smiling my brains remembered how to do their job and started to work together. They sent me a picture of Mother Theresa and one of Vincent van Gogh.

My heart and soul got the message: I will be proud to be a little like Mother Theresa together with a bit of Vincent Van Gogh: caring and creative.

I will not give up my 'rules'. This is me, I'm not giving up. I'll be the 'not fitting in' teacher, trainer, writer, coach, whatever!

Who would have thought?

My new beginning hadn't been easy, but gosh, I'm so very very glad I made this decision. I'm not running away anymore because now I know exactly who I am and I love it!
Smile, Ella

e.dejong@elladejong.com
www.elladejong.com

Heather Gallagher

When I was 18, I was diagnosed with Cone-rod degeneration. It is hereditary and many in my family had this; however my parents didn't say anything to me until my son was born. I started being super sensitive to light. I would open the front door and it was like hitting a wall: I could not see anything. My dad said "Go get your eyes checked out." So I did.

The wear and tear on my body from the pregnancy took its toll. It drew from my eyes. I had to wear dark sunglasses all the time. Light was not good for me.

I then realized I can't see to drive. I was driving my son and I around to do errands. I almost hit a semi truck head on because I didn't see it. I swerved and thank God I missed it. I had to stop driving except for little trips to the store. I lost my license when I was 21. I was having a lot of problems with my eyes changing. Nothing drastic, but very subtle. I was running into the walls, doorways, missing steps, and missing the counter. Life got a bit difficult.

We moved away from family due to my husband's job. I was starting to get a handle on my surroundings and my eyes, then my son had to start school. Ready to start over again. I had to get mobility training because, I would drop my son off at school and go and head home. I was so lost without his eyes. This was not what I wanted for my son. Mobility was very scary. I was to ride a bus and cross busy streets and yet not see what is really going on around me. I have learned that it was one of the best things I could have done for my son and I. I now have freedom to go and do what needs to be done without a driver. By the fall, my son's kindergarten year, I started having more changes in my eyes. I was getting optic migraines. My eyes would speckle up like someone turned a light on in a dark room and you have to adjust your eyes. However mine didn't go away. It took a dark room and no light to help settle my eyes. I had been dealing with all of this on my own. My husband, at the time, tried to be there for me, but made it worse. I couldn't really explain to him how I was feeling without him getting mad. I do realize now that was his coping mechanism with it all. My son understood the situation when Mommy was yelling at her eyes. He just let me be and would give me a big hug later and tell me he loved me. No matter how bad I felt, that got me through.

I wanted to work and get out into my new freedom. I went to work for the school system for about 4 years. When the program ended, I went to work at Target. I was setting aisles and stocking shelves. Then my eyes started to change again.

I was up in the rafters getting things from back stock and bringing our machine down towards the ground. It stopped, and I opened the door and went to step out and fell over 5 ft. I was okay just very bruised and sore. Thank God, but I didn't see how far I was from the ground. My depth perception had really gone away by this point. This was a little reminder: you can't see. Needless to say I didn't stay there long afterwards. I was worried that I would destroy something, hurt someone, or myself, so I quit.

My husband and I were having problems. We were in the separation process. I was feeling down on myself of who would ever want to be with me. I am legally blind and what worth am I to anyone??? Then I met my fiancé. He was so understanding, supportive, and helpful. He has dealt with, and accepted my eye situation.

I started seeing black spots in my eyes. It would come and go. However I started noticing more and more that they were not going away. I saw the doctor about it and we added on RP/ retinitis pigmentosa to the mix. There were holes in my retinas: so before I could see in the dark, now I was not seeing as well in the dark. With this came the phone call to my Uncle to let him know what was forming.

My dad and my uncle had this eye disease. They both handled things differently. My dad and I were not speaking due to divorce. Then my Uncle came back into my life after a number of years. I feel he was placed in my life then by God. He helped me more than I could ever repay him or thank him for.

He was very distant at that time, and I found out he was going through more with his eyes. He was a very proud man and didn't want others to know his battles even though he had helped me with mine. I was just looking for understanding and wanting him to know. He suggested I call my dad and let him know what was going on. This was going to be a hard phone call to make. If he was responsive, great, and if not, then he knows this is a factor in our eyes.

The best thing I could have done was call and talk to him. He felt bad and didn't know what to say. At this point, he was doing okay and his eyes were stable. However, two years after this, he had a change and sure enough he got RP too. Glad we were able to reconnect and share with each other what was happening.

My eyes have been going dark, I call it. I get an optic migraine and then one eye goes dark and the other follows it. I go to a dark room and close my eyes for about 20 minutes and all is good. If I can't get to a dark room, I close my eyes and continue with what I am doing. It is not easy all the time but, you do what you have to do. The one big thing that really helped me was calling my dad and talking to him. He understood the frustration I was going through. It is so hard to explain this to sighted people.

I then get the most dreaded call. My dad has died. I can't tell you the impact that this has had in my life. I miss him every day and wish I could call him and talk about things. He handled his eye problem with trying to run from it. Start over and maybe it would be okay. He was the man of the house and he really felt like he let his family down when he lost his vision. So he left all of us thinking we would be better off and we were far from it. I didn't realize this till many years later. Now, I wish he was still here. His death has really taken a lot out of me.

I then get a call that my Uncle had died. Only nine months after his brother died. The hardest thing about this is: he killed himself because he could not handle: the blindness. I still cry about this and pray hard that God helps me figure this out. He was a proud man. He liked being the one you go to for things and he could help. He was a good man but the darkness was too much for him to bear. I know that people say, how he could be so selfish, and hurt so many people. There are times I do understand. When I get to those low dark times, I start praying. I have to re-adjust my thinking and move forward. This death has really taken me back. It makes me question all the things we talked about, and the positive he told me to do.

I decided to write this story because of where my eyes are today. Yesterday we were doing our errands and were in a store. I had noticed my right eye go dark. I didn't say anything because, what do you do? I tried to get through the store with my left eye. I almost hit a man with a broken leg in a wheel chair with my cart. He was low and on my right side. I felt so bad. Today I got up and a big chunk of eye sight is gone. I am looking through a tunnel now on the right side. It is not painful, just frustrating. So, yes I am starting over with my vision: again. So as of today I have very limited vision on my right side, I see spots 24/7, new ones every week, and my eyes flutter all the time. It is like looking at a computer screen covered with muddy specks, and the picture is just not coming into focus.

Realizations of this eye disease: Some people want to carry this like a club; I am blind, so therefore, I am. Some people feel like it takes a part of who they are. Others feel like it takes their power away. I have seen people in my family act so differently with this. I will say, yes, I have my bad days. I cry about it, yell at it, laugh at it, and get very sad. Then I have to pick myself up and move forward. I am not dying of this, I am very blessed and love life. I know that things happen for a reason. I now turn my anxiety and stress of my eyes to God. He brings me out of the darkness and helps me put one foot in front of the other. Life is so worth living and starting over.

JENNIFER DAY

Starting Over....a new beginning

Hello, my name is Jennifer L. Day, and I am Chief Executive Officer of Daylight Media Corporation. I currently operate a very successful boutique media company, however, it was not planned this way.

I graduated college and began working in corporate finance at a fortune 500 company. I realized I had an affinity for sales, and working with people so I decided to try my hand at real estate. I fell in love with my new career immediately! I spent many incredible years being excited about closing deals and making great things happen for me and my clients! My primary focus was residential and commercial real estate. I was able to make money doing all the things I loved to do, as well as assist my clientele in achieving their goals. Life was grand!

Unfortunately, one could not predict what was about to occur in the housing market. Due to circumstances beyond my control, around the year 2008, the market took a downward spiral. As much as I hoped it would rally back, sadly it did not, and I was forced to make a completely different career change.

I decided to focus my efforts on the type of career that would give me the type of joy and passion I had with real estate. Prior to joining corporate America, I spent a lot of time immersed in the arts. I loved theater, plays, movies, music, etc. I decided to focus my efforts in that direction.

I was very fortunate to have doors opened that allowed me to hold my current position at Daylight Media. Although Daylight Media is my business, I have learned that it is necessary to take time out for my personal passions. One of my favorites is acting. I have a talent agent, take classes, book roles and work on a variety of sets as a production assistant.

I was fortunate enough to have mentors, so I'm definitely making sure I take time to give back to others. I don't let people direct my steps. I know my spirit will speak to me if I'm still. I think it is essential to be open to meeting new people, traveling, trying new restaurants, etc. It's very important to leave my "comfort zone" because one encounter can and has changed my life. Everything that has happened to me good or bad has made me extraordinarily thankful, happy, resilient and peaceful.

I have learned the art of living my truth in the present!

JENNIFER OTTS

Take the Reigns....

Thoroughbreds...such amazing, majestic, and spiritual beings of beauty. Known to most of the world, for their strength and speed, cheating in the sport of kings. Taking charge on the race track. However, the tragic part of being a thoroughbred is hitting their height, the peak of performance, early out of the gate. I, too, hit the high stakes, at a very early age, I ran hard and I ran fast, wild even, to the point that I thought I was ready to give up. After spending weeks in rehab to get clean and sober, only months later, to be diagnosed with an incurable illness, that almost killed me. Almost, but not quite.

I grew up riding horses, mustangs, stallions, barrel racing, and spending days in the woods with my best friend playing Indians, cops and robbers, and trail riding for hundreds of miles. So it was only natural that when reeling from an illness, with my future in shambles, that I turned back to my first love, riding. But I could barely even walk, due to collapsed and dead bones in my foot and ankle, much less ride. Until I met Axio, a retired racehorse. Because he had raced well, and retired early, this horse wasn't ready to be put out to pasture, kind of like me. I knew I still had greatness within me. But just like Axio, I needed a new purpose, a new job. A reason to get up and push forward.

There will always be times in life, no matter how much success, health, or wealth we achieve or amass, when we encounter a setback of some fashion. Some of those, we can plan for, and are able to offset, or bounce back from relatively pain free, but other times, we will literally, be caught off guard and hit by something so hard, so fast, that we end up on our ass, with the breathe knocked out of us. Kind of like being thrown from a horse unexpectedly. That's why sometimes in life it feels like we've just hit a brick wall from those setbacks we can't control, the ones that come out of nowhere and knock us flat on our face....like, the death of a loved one, a sudden health crisis, a divorce, a betrayal. However, I can speak from experience, a setback does not mean death, doom, or destruction of your dreams. Sometimes, landing flat on your face, doesn't mean a setback, but a set up, for an even stronger comeback. Like a racehorse that suffers an injury due to a careless jockey or trainer, just because you're off the track, doesn't mean you can't still be the winner. It may just be time for a new challenge. Every detrimental situation we suffer through, is an opportunity to rehabilitate, and retrain ourselves, for something bigger, and far better, than anything else we've known.

A perfect example from my own life is that I had a very successful real estate career that I took time away from, to help my brother get through his divorce, he had a two year old and a newborn, and as a full time father, had a very close bond with them both. Then, he suddenly died of an aortic embolism, when his girls were just two and four. At the same time I was helping him with his daughters, I got pregnant, which was an absurdly miraculous moment, because I had been told I couldn't have children due to my health, and when I got pregnant, I was on a medication that actually destroys pregnancy tissue. Because of complications from Crohn's disease and lupus, and the medications to treat them, I was a high risk pregnancy for the entire nine months. During the first ultrasound, the doctor didn't speak for almost thirty minutes, because he was in shock that I had such a healthy baby girl thriving inside my body. Then, her delivery would have made for a super suspenseful episode of a trauma baby delivery show, because she got the umbilical cord wrapped around her neck, and she had already crowned, by the time I had been prepped for an emergency c section. She was my miracle child, and her middle name is grace, because she truly is by the grace of God. It was amazing how great I felt during my pregnancy, nine blissful months of remission followed by a miraculous birth. Then the other shoe dropped, funny how that happens, right? My body began shutting down, both illnesses back with a vengeance. At one time I was on three hundred milligrams of prednisone. My blood pressure was running 110/165, stroke level.. I had an awful Crohn's disease flare that caused intestinal bleeding so severe, I needed three blood transfusions over one weekend. All of the medication, particularly prednisone, caused osteonecrosis in my left foot and ankle, which meant that all of the bones in my foot and ankle, had died. The surgeon told me all they could do, was drill decompression holes in my foot, to relieve the pain.

My first question to him, was how will I ever teach my daughter to ice skate? Or ride a bike? Or how to ride a horse? I grew up riding horses, they were my first love. My mom arranged for a horseback beach ride, and I tried to back out. But the guide was incredible, she picked out the perfect horse, named "stilettos in the sand" who quickly adjusted herself to my inabilities. That day I realized, that even though I'd been told I might be in a wheelchair for the rest of my life, I could still ride, and it gave me hope. It also gave me a new dream to work towards making a reality. I refused, from that point forward, to believe that my body couldn't heal itself, given the right tools and resources. I graduated from the Institute of Integrative Nutrition, completely changed my diet and lifestyle. I lost 65 pounds, have perfect blood pressure, and the bones in my foot and ankle have begun to heal, much to the surprise of my doctors. I've stopped taking all of the medications I was on, and my doctors have declared me not just in remission, but healed of both Crohn's disease and lupus. I adopted a rescued racehorse, named Axio, who was patient enough and willing to let me relearn how to ride. Now, I go riding every week with my daughter, and nieces, who are competing and winning horse shows. The last time my brother saw his daughters before his passing, he sat them both on their first horse. I believe that their love of horses today, is a spiritual and emotional connection and bond they have with their daddy, who is heaven. I'm blessed to be able to foster that by continuing their equestrian lifestyle, and now I'm developing my own holistic riding facility to leave as my legacy to all three girls. So I am a lot like a retired racehorse. I wasn't finished, and ready to be put in a pasture, I had a new purpose to fulfill, and new dreams to follow. What could have been a setback that put me down, I've used as a stepping stone to rise above my circumstances and live life to the fullest, everyday.

Jennifer Siller-Lasry

Designated Yarn Bowls
"Hand-Knitted Couture venues-inspired by creative outlets such as Calisthenics-to boot!"

Before I begin, I would like to acknowledge two unique individuals in whom have both given me their "Blessings"-in order to share "true feelings." Re: I have been yearning for a friend to inspire me to go back into hopes to train as a "fitness model" would train at the gym/dojo. I have been yearning for a role model, re: a true friend as someone that humbles herself and relates to me on many levels-to boot!

Re: To my dear friend Alfredo, you truly brought out my "inner shine", via enhancing an "inspirational venue", intertwined with all the venues enhanced via "creative outlets" and "calisthenics", correct? I value your work. For readers, this brilliant photographer and "Coach" for so many years and years, brought to me a renewed "sparkle", via a passion for "photography", "hand-knitted couture", and so much more…

Re: To my dear friend Elizabeth Joyce, I humbly and respectfully believe that you give "Honor", a completely renewed way to believe wholeheartedly in one of your favorite words in which is "Honesty", correct? With all due respect, thank you for the insight as to how to constantly strengthen my faith, allow me to confide in you and my yearning to assist other Veterans as yourself, via knitting venues and calisthenics; furthermore, via time to read, to meditate, to take the time to appreciate "Daily Devotions", your friendship is truly a Blessing…

On this note…

I thank you both, along with other individuals in whom I rely upon for wisdom and compassion, yet note, it is an Honor to continue knitting venues for hospice and for Veterans in whom have inspired me to appreciate everything that is as simple as where to sit under a tree and read a book to as complex as knitting dozens and dozens of hand knitted couture such as blankets and scarves, pouches and hand write as many thank you cards and letters via snail mail as possible. Thank you both for All you have done for me and continue to do; furthermore, I would like to thank other amazing pillars of strength for me and recipients as well, for All your endless efforts to support the endeavors of other volunteers as myself. Thank you for cherishing heartfelt poetry as for the opportunity to extend "heartfelt gratitude", for what you do…

Most importantly, a huge thank you to everyone that is part of my endeavors in some incredibly inspiring way via social media, in person and/or perhaps a peer, a Coach, a mentor, relative or simply a close friend. Most importantly, Blessed with the appreciation of "Daily Devotions", as for Bible Study mentors-in order to guide my steps towards "enhanced" enlightenment via published works and heartfelt poetry and essays galore in which humbled and continue to humble me…

Re: "Designated Yarn Bowls", along with other venues…

I was born on November 18th, 1979. Born in Brooklyn New York, raised in South Florida, re: Broward County, by the time I moved close to Miami Dade County back in 2003-2012, I just found knitting venues something that I left behind in my yesteryears. Re: It was not until November 18th in the year of 2003, that I realized that something important was missing in my life. Re: After discovering on November 18th or November 19th, back in 2003, some news that is hard to digest to this day, I cannot get too heavy into this area of discussion, yet it was "The Biggest discussion", with "Dad!"

To my recollection, I had to put calisthenics and mixed martial arts venues such as training in areas of martial arts and mixed martial arts on hold, while I would seek out venues such as donating time to volunteer in assisted living facilities and nursing homes as a volunteer, before choosing to work as a professional caregiver. Re: I used to work as a professional caregiver, yet I decided to work in the fashion and focus on calisthenics while I am constantly thinking of how to spend more quality time with my children. In any case, designated yarn bowls will continue to inspire me to complete each venue. In lieu of unforeseen expenses, I had to put my private lessons and gym/dojo venues on hold while I was thinking about ways to focus more on how to see "eye to eye" with my "children", and consider their needs before my own. I believe that in the future, it will truly be a "Blessing", to have my "sons", train with me at the gym/dojo of their choice. However, I would be honored to have my sons join me in my yearning to take calisthenics and mixed martial arts as in boot camp classes and all physical fitness venues more seriously. I have learned so much since February of 2015. I yearn to go back to my training immediately.

Re: On this note, it was on November 18th, whereby on every birthday, I remember when my father had given me his blessings to go back into "academic/professional" endeavors with his blessings and hope that I will continue to see to it that his grandchildren would merit from all our discussions; furthermore, "The Discussion", Re: "The Blessings" that my father had wholeheartedly given to me, before Dad had passed away on December 19th, 2003. I miss my late father and my late Grandfather as well. Re: My late Grandfather had served in the military as a proud Veteran of the U.S. Army around 1945. I had learned to twist and jive, to direct my "steps", to grandpa's tune.

Re: When my father's father, passed away in hospice in the year of 2008, I had then looked into becoming a proud knitter for hospice organizations alongside for Veterans via friends and individuals in whom have allowed me to send knitted couture and snail mail, so that others will continue to know how greatly appreciated each and every individual is to me. I must go back to thanking Mr. Alfredo and my dear friend Ms. Elizabeth Joyce, for supporting my "creative outlet" venues and allowing for me to share this "yearning" to inspire-be inspired, as for continue to inspire through the arts and through the martial arts-to boot!

Jennifer Sullivan Golubich

"Let's move south!"

My husband said those words one day while we were living in Central Ohio. We were both born and raised in the Buckeye state and were aging weary of the cold months. Well, at least I was. My parents had been deceased for almost four years, my daughter was on her way to first year of college up north and I was ready for a career upgrade with newer and warmer surroundings. I readily jumped on that invite to move.

So, South we went, with all we owned. We left family, our roots, all we had ever known. I made the long trek fun and drove with my giant plush Mickey Mouse in the front seat, to our new southern homestead. My husband landed a job in Charleston, South Carolina. I wrangled one at a local university, not far from our small "Jenga" apartment. It was smaller than most of our places we had lived at, but, I made it work. Luckily, we had storage on the same property of our apartment complex and after a few more days of purging, everything had its place. We did, too. We found favorite restaurants to frequent, beaches just twenty minutes away to escape to and obtained an enjoyable routine from errand running to washing our cars. My husband traveled for his job when it was necessary making jaunts to the airport part of our routine as well. I loved decorating our Christmas tree, the day after Thanksgiving with the patio doors open in a T-shirt, shorts, and flip flops. The history and art exposure alone in the harbor area was enough to keep me interested for years. I made some great friendships along those months. My daughter flew down on her Spring Break, from New York to thaw out and fell in love with the area, too. At night, I dodged frogs on the pavement while taking the trash out and during the day geckos clung to our screened in patio. It was an adjustment for this Yankee, but I was satisfied with sun everyday and close calls with nature. Heck, it beat scraping layers of ice off my windshield and shoveling snow in bitter temperatures like I did in the winter prior to this move.

Then one day, my husband uttered new words, "I'm getting transferred."

It turned out that the company he was working for had lost the contract they hired him on for and had an opening in Charlotte, North Carolina, come

April. I took a deep breath and agreed on another move. I tried not to let the word "North" cloud my logistical thoughts. We were still South of Ohio and warmer weather was still in our future. Again, I drove to this new homestead, with my giant plush Mickey Mouse in the front seat with me.

With this move, two and half hours away, we hired a company to pack, load, haul and unload. We found a bigger apartment to call home—quite an upgrade from our last, with a wooded area behind us filled with bird life. The time spent on the patio was so peaceful and necessary. In between getting our homestead in order, I would escape out the French doors, read my book and listen to the serenade of the birds. I could go out there until the late afternoon. I caught a nap out there from time to time, too. I unfortunately was out of a job a lot longer than I planned and when I did start my job at the local university, I immensely missed my patio time and singing friends. This local university, which didn't seem all that local, had me trek almost thirty miles away from home to fill their new position in a department I again, slipped into well. I loved my hour lunch time in the beautiful outdoors till about November. Nature was still attracted to me as I fed a few cardinals and squirrels from the umbrella covered bench area. My coworkers and the students we assisted became my new family.

We fell into our routines here, too. I loved that we were so close to the South Carolina border so I could still feel more "South" at brief moments when it came to errands—even washing the cars. Again, we favored some certain restaurants, the local botanical garden and even a minor baseball team to cheer on. More friendships developed and I started to feel my creative niche grounded, as I started teaching at a local art guild facility. I even placed in an art show at the library in our area. Then it happened again. New words from my husband I never wanted to here.

"We're moving back."

It was now the end of December in 2016 and we were heading back to Ohio. My mind couldn't make sense of this. Ohio was not my definition of South. I remember my sister trying to bring comfort to my boggled logistical thinking by saying, "Well, you are still South....in Ohio." It's all she had and it's all I had too, to make it still seem…South.

I packed up all my personal belongings. I purged physically and emotionally.

Friends were baffled. Family was elated. Me? Exhausted.

We now reside on the west side of Cincinnati, Ohio. I am the Communications and Building Operations Coordinator at a Presbyterian church. The organ music that echoes from the sanctuary down the halls of the building to my office to the bell tolls on the hour, reminds me daily as to where I am. It's not the hustle and bustle of a university atmosphere at a community desk or the stuffy out of date building demanding my time from a desk in the center of a drafty lobby. I had moved to an office, a place to call my own, with a door that locks.

Soon after I was accepted for the position, an elder of the church found everlasting peace and passed away. The Monday after the funeral, I noticed a huge daisy floral arrangement at the front desk. The one volunteer said it was a unique one since many don't use daisies for funerals. Daisies always warmed my heart, because my Mom grew them. At my mother's funeral, we picked some from her garden and placed them by her. To many it was an extra floral arrangement sitting pretty at the desk, but, to me it was a beautiful sign from my mother that she approved of where I was. She approved of me starting over--here.

To me the words *"Let's move south"* clearly translated to *"Let's start over."* Starting over three times in two years was not what I planned to do when I agreed to moving south, let alone take residence close to the place where I started from. Through all the packing, unpacking, reorganizing, familiarizing, and abandoning, it was a very stressful, unpredictable time for me. I learned I can adjust very well to reestablishing myself no matter what climate, city or position. I learned, to notice the signs along the way, too. See everyone, starting over can be done. Look at me-- I did it-- again, again, and AGAIN!

South Carolina or Bust!

JILL O'BRIEN

Horses and racing have always been a focal point of my life. I was fortunate to grow up in Cork, Ireland with my parents owning a racetrack on our property while they were heavily involved in other aspects of the industry. Ponies were at the center of my childhood and growing up, I was immersed into all equestrian facets such as show jumping, eventing, hunting, and started galloping racehorses when I was 11. There was no escaping it, and I was hooked.

When I was 12, I was diagnosed with Leukemia, which required 2 years of chemotherapy. A few complications with medication restricted my walking greatly, and I was on crutches for over 12 months waiting for my immune system to strengthen so I could undergo surgery. But, because, I couldn't ride our ponies, I didn't want anything to do with them. It was too hard for me to only be half involved in something that my entire childhood had revolved around. It was on my doorstep, literally. I didn't know how to not be involved, and I made the decision to sell my pony, Lady.

Fast forward to my late teens, early 20's. Thankfully, I was fully recovered, and fully mobile again. I studied and graduated from Arts at University College Cork, and in 2010, I did my first J1 summer in Manhattan, and boarded at New York University Dorms (yes, my address was 35, 5th Avenue!) With that address, I sure got my first taste for the Big Apple....

At 21, upon graduating, I moved to Dublin in search for work. I built my resume and my career in my six years there. I pursued my passion and went back to study and graduate from Communication Studies at Dublin City University. Returning to college at 23 was a tough decision but proved to be a hugely beneficial one. I'm definitely not one for regrets but not having chosen to do a media course in college first time around always niggled at me. I think I always knew that I'd end up working with horses. But television, no. In many ways, I think that chose me and my teenage experience shaped my career.

My periodic time spent in recovery, usually in strict isolation wards, forced me to be entertained solely by television, as visitors were denied access, and even board-games were sometimes banned due to risk of germs. I became captivated by film and its ability to transport you to another world.

I went on to study further at the renowned Park Studios in Dublin and my mentor advised me to specialize in what I know, but most of all, to specialize in what I was passionate about. Insert horse racing. During my time at DCU, I sought various internships at horse racing companies, including the Racing Post Newspaper and the Irish Point-To-Point website. These proved invaluable, and allowed me to wet my feet in the primary stages of my career.

During the Summers of 2013, and 2014, I traveled to New York again, on J1 Visa's. I lived the hectic, fun, Manhattan lifestyle. In between, I volunteered at the Double H Ranch Camp in New York, which is an activity camp for seriously ill children. I had attended its sister camp, Barretstown, in Ireland, when I was ill, and I had continued to volunteer there throughout my twenties, and occasionally exercised their horses on the weekends. Both years, I also attended Saratoga track season with a jockey friend and did photography on the backstretch in the morning time, and attended the races afterwards. I fell in love with Saratoga and American horse racing.

I had every intention in returning to New York in the of Summer of 2015, on my final J1 Summer visa. However, I was chosen for a prestigious marketing and events internship at Horse Racing Ireland. I had to take this opportunity, and New York had to wait. I was based at Leopardstown Racecourse, Ireland's premier track which hosts a Summer long festival with a combination of horse racing, fashion awards, and music festivals. It gave me my first insight into the logistics of planning major events weekly, liaising with the media, celebrity guests, and actively thinking outside the box in terms of digital marketing. My contract was extended to assist in marketing the international recognized Irish Champions Weekend. I had worked at a restaurant part-time throughout that internship, finishing at Leopardstown at 5pm and starting at 6pm at the restaurant with minutes to do a change of uniform, attitude, and mind frame.

While working one night at the restaurant, I was serving two gentlemen who were in Dublin from Hollywood, working on a movie, called I.T, starring Pierce Brosnan and Anna Friel. We spoke about my experience and degree they asked me to work on the movie with them, as their PA. I (painfully) declined and explained my predicament with my then current internship. So, we made a compromise. I was to play an extra in the movie. I spent three days shooting and hanging out with Pierce Brosnan, (in between my other two jobs!) and I watched myself in the movie last Fall from my couch in New York. Surreal!

I finished working at Leopardstown, and was back waitressing full-time. Two weeks later, I got a phone call from Horse Racing Ireland's HQ at The Curragh Racecourse, and was offered a job in Ownership and Horse Registrations. I leapt at the job opportunity even though it was 70km from where I lived, and I had no car… But, I made it work! I enjoyed a flip side of the industry working with the main players and investors in the game until April 2016…. And, on May 6th, 2016, I jetted to New York on a 12-month Graduate Visa.

I went through fazes of thinking I was daft leaving, that I was abandoning everything I had worked for in Ireland, but I knew it was what I truly wanted. I boarded that Aer Lingus flight to the concrete jungle with a suitcase, a bunch of resumes and a (very!) hopeful mind. It was the turning point of my career, and I struck luck.

Three days after I landed on American turf, I started work with the New York Racing Association television department as their Production Assistant. I was based at Belmont Park Racetrack until mid-July, then moved to Saratoga for the 7-week track season there, and back to Belmont in September through October for the Fall meeting.

I worked on NYRA's live TV shows, which were broadcasted on Fox Sports 2, and MSG. We had five, 2-hour, live shows a week, sometimes 3-hour shows. In the mornings, I assisted the producer with the segment rundown of the show, researching content, and analyzing racing statistics for our viewers while also assisting in shooting and editing video content. During the show, I was reporter, Maggie Wolfendale's, assistant. I was between the paddock and the winner's circle, lining up interviewees, and everything in between. I loved how I got to interact with the connections of the horses, and listen to Maggie analyze some of the best horses and races in the country. The most mesmerizing people that I pre-interviewed were Barry Schwartz of Calvin Klein, Vinnie Viola of Florida Panthers, Hall of Famer, Mike Smith, and Chef, Bobby Flay. This is not taking from the fact that I worked with incredible stars every day, these stars were my colleagues, the talent, the production team, the hall of fame trainers, and jockeys, the list goes on…

In between, I was Stage Manager for NBC Sports on Stars and Stripes Day at Belmont Park and worked alongside, horseback reporter, Donna Brothers.

During Saratoga, I worked for NYRA's Press Department. This involved watching and dissecting workouts in the mornings, going from barn to barn interviewing trainers, and regurgitating it all into a press release by midday. From there, I interviewed winning jockeys and trainers post-race, and combined my information with my team to do a write-up for the website at the end of the day. A highlight was having my article published in the race program on Whitney Weekend and my photography in the Travers' Magazine.

After Belmont Fall meet, I traveled to Santa Anita, California, for eight days to work as television stage manager for the 2016 Breeders' Cup. I started work at 6am with the HRTV crew, and worked on their show, and from there worked on the daily simulcast show. During the two days of the Breeders' Cup Festival, I managed six reporters and worked with European reporters including Olli Bell and Emma Spencer. It was the most exhilarating and enlightening experience to date. I lived in Hollywood while I managed one of the biggest stages in the world. I stood in the winner's circle with the record breaker, Arrogate. After my eight days there, I caught a flight back to JFK with the champ, Richard Migliore, and I never felt so thankful for every single opportunity that had come my way and what I had achieved.

I'm a firm believer in saying yes to every shot that comes your way, you can always make it work; there's always more coffee. It's important to embrace hard work; it will be recognized and rewarded. I have found the one job which allows me to use my academic knowledge and practical skills while pursuing my passion in the industry and the city that I adore.
New York, my horse jungle, where dreams are made of….. That's my winning trifecta.

JoDee Kenney

From Top Story to True Meaning

His tiny cry was the most beautiful, precious, glorious, startling announcement of his arrival into our world. Through tears, I kept begging my husband to answer my question *"Donavan! What did we do?! What did we do?"* My husband looked up to me through his tears and said "Awe, Joseph." In an instant, my definition of love went from black and white to a brilliant rainbow of colors. Joseph introduced me to emotions I didn't even know existed. Seconds before Joseph's arrival, I didn't know I could love so completely, and I was not sure about my chosen path. And yet, it was now clear I found my destiny. That was September 7th, 2002, my moment I started over and learned there was no doubt — I was meant to be a mom.

My path to parenthood almost didn't happen. Rewind a year to 2001. I was a hard-driving, working woman with a high-pressure career as a Television News Anchor/Reporter in Louisville, Kentucky. I loved my job. I was the first to volunteer to go out on breaking news. When I wasn't at work, I was watching the news at home. I was the girl who would eat, drink and sleep news. I had aspirations to be a national correspondent. Then came a fateful day that would change my course.

September 11, 2001, started out like any other. I was sitting at my desk reading the newspaper and listening to a morning news show when an alert came over the wires. A small plane hit a building in New York City. I turned to the TV, and the national news anchors announced a special report. As soon as I saw the live picture of the World Trade Center building on fire I said: "That building is going to come down." Several people didn't believe it could happen. As we all know now, it wasn't a small plane but a large passenger jet that hit the World Trade Center. Then a second plane hit the other tower, and they both came tumbling down. Another aircraft struck the Pentagon, and a fourth came down in a field in Pennsylvania. Terror gripped the nation.

We looked to the sky and feared any jet that seemed to be flying too low until an eerie silence came over our skies and we didn't see any at all. I remember driving to the Pentagon with my photographer, and for hours we felt unsettled to not see a plane in sight. While my husband worried at home all alone, I didn't think twice as I headed toward the story. At that moment I felt it was my duty to tell people what happened.

We spent a week reporting from the Pentagon in the wake of 9-11. We talked with people who lost loved ones. We captured images of fire reigniting in the charred structure. We recorded patriotic firefighters draping a giant American flag on the side of the building. All of these stories were touching, but I was stoic. I felt numb and thought I was able to compartmentalize my concerns pretty well. It was not until moments before my last live appearance from the scene that my emotions hit me.

I was waiting for my colleague reporting from New York City to introduce me when someone in his background caught my eye. A person was holding a picture of a loved one, desperately shaking the image so people would see it on the news. In an instant, I locked in on the anguish and heartbreak of that moment in our history. I realized it wasn't the event I was reporting on, it was humanity. 9-11 brought out the worst of some people and the best in more. I was reporting on the tension between horrible acts of destruction, desperate acts of love and heroic acts of selflessness. I began to cry. I was snapped out of my thoughts when I heard my producer say "JoDee, stand by." It was almost time for my live report. I somehow composed myself and got through telling my last story from the Pentagon.

The following few weeks were a blur. Life got back to a new normal. People went back to work. The news continued to happen. But something inside me had changed. I began to question the true meaning of life, why I was so committed to my career and wondered if there was more to my existence. I asked myself the cliche question "At the end of your life will your news director be there mourning you and your life's work?" The answer was "I doubt it." I thought a lot about that person shaking the picture into the camera in New York City and wondered if they found their loved one. I thought about the importance of family. I thought about how worried my husband was when I carelessly packed a bag and ran to the Pentagon, chasing the big story. I secretly thought about starting a family.

When I finally admitted to my husband that I wanted to start a family, he was so excited. After ten years of marriage, I think he may have given up on the idea. We immediately got pregnant, and nine months later we were at the moment when my life started over. The birth of my son Joseph was like a door bursting open to a part of my heart I didn't even know I had. He was the missing piece to my puzzle, the north to my compass. I thought my destiny was to become a hard-charging journalist. In fact, my destiny was to become a mom. I now have achieved my intended destiny with three beautiful children. Joseph, Trinity, and Anyssa taught me to be selfless, caring, and compassionate. They have brought me endless joy, taught me to be introspective, and helped me realize there is so much more to life.

It is hard to think that such beauty can be born from such tragedy, but I am humbly thankful for the experience just the same. While I am living the life I was meant to live; I am also performing the job I love with more compassion and understanding. I have the best of both worlds: motherhood and a meaningful career. I now have a deeper understanding of people's perspectives. While reporting the news, I truly want to understand what motivates, and inspires people to speak with me.

At the end of my day, I go home to my loving family that continues to inspire me to live my best life. I look in my children's eyes and see a future filled with hope, optimism, and joy. They let me know that my existence matters and motivate me to set a positive example to follow. I hope I can also be an example to others that seeking your true destiny will bring you insurmountable joy. I can genuinely say that I love my life. Thanks to my children I am more grateful for my life and hope I serve as an inspiration to others that starting over can be complex and bewitching and worth the journey.

http://www.facebook.com/JoDeeKenneyNews
Twitter: @JoDeeKenney

JOHN POLO

I am starting over. Again.

I have started over before as a result of her.

Michelle. My amazing wife.

The first time at the age of seventeen. When our teenage romance began. And I fell madly in love with her.

The second time at the age of eighteen. When she ended it with me. And broke my heart.

The third time at the age of twenty six. When we reunited. And we realized that the love previously shared had never went away.

And then, there was the fourth time.

The fourth time that I started over.

She, was thirty years young.

I was thirty one years, old.

January 22, 2016.

The day that she died in my arms.

So much of our history, I vividly remember. From the day that I first noticed how beautiful she was, to the day that I first realized her physical appearance –as jaw dropping as she was, paled into comparison to her inner beauty.

I miss her.

I miss her in our youth. The teenage romance that made a young man fall madly in love with his blonde beauty. Those memories I will forever cherish.

I miss her in our past. The reuniting of soul mates after nearly a decade apart. A fairytale romance I will never forget.

I miss her in our future. Fifty beautiful years together. Stolen from us in the most callous of ways.

The truth is, she is what I always wanted. The only woman I ever loved, even during our nearly decade apart.

Michelle and I enjoyed one year together as teenagers, followed by eight years apart. We enjoyed five years together as adults, until death did us part.

There is was one additional 'restart' in the history of John and Michelle that I did not mention before.

The day that she was diagnosed.

July 22, 2013.

Michelle fought valiantly.

She fought valiantly against the raging beast inside of her, for two and a half long years.

January 22, 2016.

Surrounded by family, friends and love, this would be the day that Michelle would take her last breath with us. After an epic battle with one of the most rare and aggressive cancers known to man.

The simple truth is, I never thought I could do it.

Start over.

Without her.

The raw truth is, I hadn't planned on doing it.

Start over.

Without her.

I had planned on joining her.

The thought of losing my entire family, too much to bear.

I did not join her though.

I am here.

Starting over.

With an exhausted mind, a shattered heart and a devastated soul, I somehow picked myself up, I somehow dusted myself off, and I somehow began anew.

In the most tragically ironic of ways, my new life – without my love – began in hospice, as her life was coming to an end.

It is there, that I picked up my laptop and began to write. The words popping off my fingertips so quickly that I could barely maintain pace.

What began as an honorable duty, now a roaring passion I can hardly contain.

Her eulogy. A work of love, for a woman who deserved such a fitting good bye.

My book. The tale of our love story, one that is equally full of beauty and heartache.

It was there, that I realized that although I may no longer be a husband, my role as a step dad to Michelle's amazing daughter would continue. A role that I cherish, above all else.

My heart full of love for two.

My wife, and my step daughter.

It was there, that I realized that some form of good can come from even the most intense of pains.

I listened to her.

I listened to Michelle. The single strongest person I have ever known.

She told me to be strong. She told me that I could do it. She told me that I could make it through.

She told me she knew that I could. She told me that she believed that I would.

Here I stand.

Starting over, because of her.

Because of HER.

Because of her words. Because of her strength. Because of her belief in me. Because of her love for me.

Today, after experiencing hell on Earth, I can honestly say - that I am a new man.

I am a better man.

The bitterness, gone.

The appreciation, found.

The purpose, discovered.

I am here, to share my story. To share our story. I am here, to strip way the layers of self-protective armor worn by us all, to share my grief and expose my soul. Not because I think in some grand way that I am going to change the world, but because if I can help one person, for them the world has been changed.

I am here, to love Michelle. In death, just as I did in life.

I am here, to carry on her legacy. For her. For me. For all of us.

Most importantly, I am here to be a step dad. To be the best step dad that I can be. To devote my life to the true love of Michelle's life. Her little girl. So that she knows she is loved, always. So that she knows her mother is with her, always. So that I can give her every chance she deserves to live a happy and healthy life. Just as Michelle so wanted me to do.

Loving Michelle. Taking care of Michelle. Loving her daughter. Taking care of my step daughter. These were, and are, the greatest honors of my life.

I am here, for a future. Whatever that future may be.

Love again, in time, I hope will find its way.

Success, health and happiness – all the possibilities, because I gave myself another day.

I did not ask for this journey. I certainly did not ask for this fate.

I am here though.

Starting over.

'Me', sadly – instead of 'We'.

One day I'll see her again.

Until then, starting over is what it shall be.

You can find John Polo on his blog page at www.betternotbitterwidower.com or on Facebook by searching Better Not Bitter Widower

My love.

KATHLEEN KOHLER SCHWARTZ

Our wedding was a picture from a fairytale book. We were two teens who fell crazy in love with each other in high school. He joined the Navy and I aspired to be the perfect wife and mother.

Two months later, the honeymoon began to change…quickly. There was a dark side I had not seen in the two years we dated. One day, we had a disagreement over stocking the kitchen cabinets, and he forcefully back-handed me across the stomach. I warned him that if he ever struck me again, I would leave. But I justified to myself that he was having a bad day. This was foreign territory for me.

Life moved on. The next year, we celebrated the birth of our first child, Patricia. My husband adored her and played with her every chance he could. But, with added responsibilities, he soon became more abusive – this time in his language- and soon after, some questionable behavior with a minor girl. I didn't know what to do, I was only nineteen years old. I was in shock. When I asked about the girl, he dismissed my concerns and said I was jealous. This incident left another checkmark in my mental list that something was amiss.

Within 2 years, we moved to Cherry Point, North Carolina. Child number two was due within a month of our move. My husband immediately began field medical training in Camp Lejeune, about an hour south of our home base. As most military wives do, I quickly made friends with our neighbors and set up "camp" with sitters and offer help, as well.

Our firstborn son, Matthew, was born on time. He was a beautiful boy. 24 hours later, I was alerted that his internal organs were not developed. Due to limited facilities, he was taken by helicopter to Portsmouth, Virginia Naval Base hospital.

My son's life was spared through the expertise of an *adult* surgeon who risked his livelihood to save my child. He and I prayed by his bedside for a miracle. While I stayed at the hospital for a week, friends cared for my two year old at home. My husband, however, did not fare well in this tragedy. He tried to find fault; and, laid with multiple women to ease his pain, as he informed me later.

When Matthew was diagnosed with Cystic Fibrosis, we were awarded a discharge from the military so we could get help from doctors at home in St. Louis. Matthew's multiple daily treatments, ostomy care, and close supervision were required to sustain his life expectancy of two years old.

Life seemed to become normal for us, yet the abuse was like a sucker punch. Name calling, cursing, screaming, being pushed up against the wall with his knee to my groin. Yet, in a fleeting moment of grief (my grandfather died), we had one intimate moment, and child number three was born nine months later.

Returning home from work, early one day, I saw a strange pair of shoes under my coffee table with two wine glasses. Upon the woman gathering her wares and leaving sheepishly, I gave my husband the choice of his family or this woman. He chose the latter, and left our house that afternoon, never to return.

The decision to divorce and strike out on my own was a huge change for me. I grew up in a family where the mom took care of the kids, held backyard birthday parties, and sipped iced tea with the neighborhood moms while the kids played. I was devastated. I felt I had failed my family, failed my children and mostly failed myself.

I took my husband's belongings, threw them in the back of the pick-up truck and drove it downtown to her business where they worked together. Mind you, I had to hot-wire the truck to start it. Yeah, that's right.

As I parked in the lot, I don't know where my mental or physical strength came from, but I hopped up on the bed of the truck, unloaded all of his clothes, trophies and guns and threw them in front of the door of her business. She was standing at the window, hands on her hips, yelling, "I'm going to call the police on you." I responded, "Go ahead, and you will be on the docket for a lawsuit right behind the divorce case!"

An onlooker, stepped forward, smiled at me, and began to clap his hands, as though I gave a star performance. I bowed in return, hopped in the truck and headed back home to my children.

That day, I left and never looked back. I chose freedom – for my children, and for me. I felt that if I could put a roof over our head and food in our stomachs, life was okay. There were other women who had it worse, I would remind myself.

Change was good. It came at a cost, but I was grateful for the surprises it brought. We were poor, no doubt. I sold the pickup for money to get an apartment, and my brother lent me his beater car with missing floorboards and a rear windshield that shook each time you drove over 40 miles per hour.

I landed a job at a home health agency as a manager. Every day I stepped out of my beater car in a suit and high heels. I was proud to be able to work and support my children as best I could.

Without a college degree, I worked through the ranks of the healthcare industry and was promoted to regional management in the final years of my corporate career. I recognized that *change* was a journey that I came to appreciate.

These seemingly difficult times were rich gifts that not everyone gets to experience. They were meant for me and only me. What I learned from these tragic moments was up to me. I chose freedom, to find my wisdom, and mentor those who seek the same.

Facebook: https://facebook.com/taprootsforlife/
LinkedIn: https://www.linkedin.com/in/taprootsforlife
Instagram: https://www.instagram.com/taprootsforlife/
Twitter: https://twitter.com/taprootsforlife
Wordpress.com: https://taprootsofwisdom.wordpress.com
Meetup: https://www.meetup.com/Taproots-for-Life/
Tumbler: taprootsforlife.tumblr.com
beBee: https://www.bebee.com/bee/taprootsforlife
ReferralKey: referralkey.com/taprootsforlife

Katherine Carlson-Penley

Great Big Canvas

Ever stop to wonder what your choices were as a high school student when planning your life? Guidance Counselors showing you large paperback catalogs of college degree courses, introduction of financial aid, college campus summaries, and the endless application forms necessary to be considered as a college student. Emotions are high with excitement, worry, nervous jitters, and stress all due to the fact that this is one of the biggest tests a teenager takes before graduating high school to live in the adult world.

When my father was about to retire from the United States Navy in 1973, we settled in Ellsworth, Maine, which is near the magnificent and beautiful Acadia National Park located in Bar Harbor, Maine. Living in Ellsworth in the 1970s was a small, quaint, and safe town where doors were unlocked, children of all ages played outside with other children in neighborhoods from sunrise to suppah-time and if a ride was needed, there was always someone close by to help.

Each person in this World strives to be successful in one way or another but there are others who strive to find their one destiny and meaning in their own lives. There is a phrase that I go by which is *There is an Old Path at the End of the Rainbow*. Life gives choices by way of Paths that are chosen but there is only One Path destined for each person and it is up to that individual to find that One Path which provides complete Passion and Peace in Life.

During my high school years, I was lazy in thinking what I wanted to do after graduation. During this trying and nervous time, I was a typical teenager more interested in the teen magazines of Tiger Beat and 16 Special, listening to my record albums including music on single 45s, dancing in our family basement, and television. The only downfall to television back then was if the president was on all three channels, you were screwed or be stuck watching something on the PBS channel. I was a very shy young girl who was always nervous around kids my own age as well as crowds in public places. I grew habits of watching and listening to students in the school hallways between classes wondering if they were talking behind my back or some silly thing. Learning in classrooms was a challenge for me because no matter where my assigned seat was, it was always near students distracting other students that were there to learn. But there was one classroom that I enjoyed very much because it was a place where I felt safe with no distractions. It was Art Class. The room smelled of oil and acrylic paints, was messy with different size canvases scattered around the room and the tables had their own art form from students learning how to paint. When I stepped into the classroom, I was transformed into a different world, a different culture, a place to be myself without any regard to peer pressure. There was Passion and Peace. Painting and drawing have always been a love of mine since I was very young and when I turned eight-years-old, I remember one of my aunts asking me what I wanted to be when I grew up. I told her I wanted to be an artist. I loved to paint with acrylic because this medium was not restrictive and it dried quickly giving me more time to add unlimited layers of detail on the canvas. I took two years of art classes in high school learning movement and position of lines, the endless encouragement in thinking the impossible and thinking outside the box by creating anything on canvas. What I learned from those two years helped prepare me in my later years by creating beautiful acrylic paintings on canvases where movement is 'felt and seen' – Clouds move in the sky while the waves of the ocean pound against the rocky coastline and the beautiful fragrance aroma of flowers fill the air. I knew I wanted to be a full-time artist; I just had to figure out how to get to that One Path.

As graduation approached in June 1980 and no decision made of a career choice, I had to decide quickly what I wanted to do so after discussing with my parents that I wanted to attend an art school. It was decided that I should search an alternative career because there was a possibility that I would not be able to support myself as an artist. Art careers in the 1970s were scarce compared to today's society, and I felt crushed in setting aside earning an art degree to find a more stable career. I honestly had no idea what to do but one thing I did not want was office work as I felt it did not provide creativity or enough challenge to work as a life-long career. The career I chose was my second passion - Travel and Tourism. Being a Navy Brat living in other States and countries learning different cultures, I felt this was a decent choice to work and save money by selling my artwork on the side and also have fun traveling the World using the travel benefits. I worked for Bar Harbor Airlines/Eastern Airlines/Continental Airlines for nearly 10 years gaining experience in ticketing, marketing and analysis, and just having fun before being furloughed when Continental Airlines filed Chapter 11 in the early

1990s. This was the only employment I had in the travel industry and came to realize this was a time to sit down and seriously decide what I wanted to do with my life.

Fast-forward to the current year – 2017 – I am 54 years old and in the past year, have had many conversations with *me, myself, and I* asking why I have not reached my goal as a full-time artist. For 35 years, I have worked in administrative office positions in different industries that provided stability, experience and opportunities to *Climb the Corporate Ladder* and through those years, having gone through three furloughs (employment layoffs) and one recession. During these years, I felt something inside me was missing – I did not feel complete. Even though I am proud of my accomplishments and received countless recognitions of positions I worked in, they were not satisfying to me because there was no creativity in the work to enjoy like the feeling of an art piece on a wall at home that you love to look at because it makes you feel happy or it brings peace within you. I wanted to create paintings in a workshop.

I have a business called <u>Scenic Artwork of New England</u>. I love to create original acrylic paintings of New England sceneries and specialize in custom original art work on canvases. You know how a book tells a story? Paintings tell a story also. It explains the emotional energy the artist felt when creating the art piece, a journey mesmerized. This energy is what drives me to put as much detail on the canvas. After recovering from an automobile accident in 1997, I established this company while living and working in Maine continuing with the business in New Hampshire where I currently reside. I created a Facebook Page of the business titled Scenic Artwork of New England which gives viewers a chance to look at my acrylic artwork and the page also includes original color pencil on sketch pad paper. I am currently writing a Business Plan to finally work as a full-time Owner and Artist. Learning new business strategies in marketing, communication, customer service and website design are challenging but exciting at the same time. I believe new opportunities are around the corner and many doors are open to create and sell more paintings of coastline sceneries, wildlife, and special places of family homes/properties from customer requests.

I read an article a few years ago about Danny Kaye, Entertainer, and one phrase that he said caught my eye.

'Life is a Great Big Canvas. Throw all the paint on it you can.'

Life has so many opportunities that even though obstacles appear at the most unusual times, there is always a second chance to start something new and roll with it. The Path is there waiting to be walked on; the greatest satisfaction is approaching it.

Starting over by finally taking charge of my career is uplifting because I feel this is another second chance for a new beginning. A beginning on a journey where Peace and Passion abound with different styled white canvases and magical brushes in a messy yet peaceful art room. Reaching my One Path has raised my confidence and endless amounts of energy, and I look forward to sharing my love of artwork with others.

KATIE GORHAM

I've always been an optimist, finding the good in everything, at times even to a fault. Positivity has gotten me through a lot in my life so far. Through the years I've transitioned well in times of inevitable adaptability. Change and uncertainty has remained a constant. Despite occasional moments of poor judgement, I found myself adjusting with grace, at least on the outside. I wish I had a dime for every time someone commented on my happy and enthusiastic attitude. It wasn't until these last few years that I understood what the saying "happiness is a choice" meant. Being my usual, charismatic and happy-go-lucky self became a serious challenge. When I began to notice the good days, because they were so few and far between, I knew I had reached that point, the point where I had allowed all the struggles and adversity that I had faced to consume me. Whether or not I was still bothered by issues of the past, my ability to be the strong one was quickly fading. Throughout my adulthood I've endured a lot without much help. It was never intentional for me to cope alone. I remember the first few times I talked about what was bothering me and those I spoke to were compassionate, but didn't really know how to respond. They were either shocked and remorseful, or asked me why I wasn't doing more to help. The problem is, there wasn't anything I could do to help. It took a lot of time and emotional strife for me to really understand that it was completely out of my hands.

When a colleague of mine starting working on a multi platform project and conversation about heroin in the community, I thought the time had come for me to share my experience with loving a heroin addict, loving two addicts actually. I've rehearsed my story over and over in my mind, but up until now I have never allowed those thoughts to become spoken or written words. 400 miles away, in my hometown of Harpers Ferry, West Virginia, it wasn't just old friends and high school classmates who were succumbing to heroin addiction, the epidemic hit my home, my flesh and my blood, and it hit relentlessly hard.

They say it's a blessing and a curse to feel so much, and I wholeheartedly agree. Maybe it's a symptom of being the oldest child, but I've always strived to be a positive force in my siblings' lives. Despite any insecurities or unhappiness I've felt in my life, I've always felt my best self when around my family. When it became a reality that two of my younger sisters, who also happen to be identical twins, were getting involved with hard drugs, it made me question so much about myself and my actions. Had I been a bad influence? What could I have done differently growing up? If I was at home with my family, would this have happened? Not only had I gained an incredibly heavy weight on my shoulders, but I became increasingly paranoid and feared the worse each and every day.

The story of "The Boy Who Cried Wolf" took on a new meaning to my family. Every time I was told this would be the last time, I believed them. Continuously getting your hopes up has repercussions. It was emotionally exhausting. I didn't know who or what to believe anymore, especially when they'd lie about one another to look better themselves. It could just be pressure I've put on myself, but for a long while I've felt like the glue that has held my family together, despite my physical distance. Consoling my mother over the phone became a part of my daily routine. As chaos became the norm for my family, I found myself numb and not present. I would get lost in my memories, the one place where I knew I could always find my sisters.

Until one is completely ready for recovery, I've found that jail or death are the only viable options for a heroin addict. When my sisters found themselves incarcerated, I admittedly felt a sense of relief because I knew where they were. When stints in and out of jail weren't rock bottom enough, hopelessness ensued yet again. What was it going to take? Did one of them have to die for the other to wake up? For years I grieved for people who were no longer alive, physically alive, but hardly living. I had lost my God given friends and it created a sense of emptiness I could not overcome.

As an optimist I grew up with the notion that everything happened for a reason, but I could not bring myself to understand or accept why this was happening. It seems as if a generation of people were being laid to rest in my hometown. It is by the grace of God that my family has not had to plan a funeral. Despite that, I wouldn't say we have come out of this unscathed. An orange jumpsuit was one of my sister's outfit for the vast majority of her early twenties. My other sister had become a mother during that period of time, and it seemed as if she had integrated sobriety into her life quite well. The phone call I received on February 10th, 2015 proved otherwise. Two months shy of my niece's first birthday, my sister had relapsed and overdosed. The details of that day continue to rock me to my core. I left work early to provide my mother support from a distance as she waited to receive news of whether or not the overdose was fatal. Upwards of nine other people that day lost their lives to the same batch of heroin my sister used. As the story is told, she was lying in the grass on the side of the road after becoming unresponsive in the passenger's seat. Multiple people surrounded her, doing nothing, with my other sister (not in jail at the time) screaming for someone to help. A man had pulled up to the scene, performed CPR and got my sister breathing again. She quite literally, met her guardian angel, Thomas, that day. Knowing how that day could of turned out continues to give me chills today. A constant reminder at how precious life is.

The time that has passed between then and now, hasn't been the most harmonious. My grandmother passed away not knowing why two of her grandchildren had been absent. For years I wondered if it was shame that prevented my father from telling his parents the truth. It's a conversation I certainly don't take lightly, and it wasn't until this past fall that I confided in my grandfather and told him what my father had been neglecting to share. A censored conversation it was. I didn't go into detail about the overdose or scenarios that had played out of the years, but I told him the truth, the reasons why they had been so out of touch. It wasn't the first time I shared tears with my granddad. I've tried to understand the reasons my dad has for not telling his parents, but at the end of the day, for me at least, family is everything. My family is my everything, and I didn't want any more secrets.

My story, of being the loved one of two addicts, is far from over. Sobriety and recovery is currently a reality for my sisters, but I find myself fearing that I will lose them again. Living in fear is no way to live, and it's something I'm working on, being that optimistic person again, trusting that we are all where we are supposed to be. No matter how many times they tell me they are fine, there's that voice in the back of my head, knowing how quickly it can be taken away again. There's so much to be thankful for and not take for granted, the ability to communicate with them on a regular basis, and being together for the holidays. Seeing their health and happiness restored has allowed me to personally heal. Moving forward hasn't always been an easy task, but with Aimee and Amanda in my life, everyday we have we are given the chance for a new beginning.

KEITH LANE

They Can't Take Away Our Creativity

After another long day on the road, the mind races.

In September of 2008, the first industry red-lined in the recession
was advertising. Over 130,000 talented individuals were dumped like trash.

Many of us lost everything. Everything. And these were people
with extraordinary skills. What you first learn is who your real friends are.
They helped in any way they could.

Personally, I applied for graveyard shifts washing dishes, cleaning hotel
toilets,
and unloading trucks, only to be told I was overqualified and dismissed.
I searched trash barrels for bottles and cans to deposit so I could purchase
crackers and water.

That was me, the guy who helped build a global ad agency.

By day, I scratched out nickel and dime freelance jobs to survive.
No car. No nothing.

My good friend Erik Proulx made an inspirational documentary titled
Lemonade.
It focused on the recession's devastating effect on the advertising industry,
and how creative professionals were reinventing themselves to embark on a
positive new future.

Erik didn't charge admission as he knew we were all broke.
It was an incredible evening. A homecoming of sorts to be with my ad
friends.
People I worked with were featured in this honest, heartfelt, and moving
film.

Erik asked me to write a review. I was honored.

These were my words:
"They can take away our material possessions, but they can't take away our creativity. We own that, and it is our property."

It has been 9 years since then.

We have been coming back strong and seeing the light again.
-Keith Lane
Founder, Partner, Creative Director of Arnold Fortuna Lane & Cabot
(now Arnold Worldwide)
www.klanecd.com

Kristen Maslanka

The Tortoise Win's the Race

I recently cut my hair. I'd never done it myself, and I only needed a trim. For years I had been eagerly awaiting a visit to the salon but it just didn't fit in with the schedule. So there I was desperate enough to stand in front of the mirror with a pair of scissors to my hair. With anxiety stringing through my veins, I snipped.

Just like that, no satisfaction, no significant change, the hair just fell to the floor unceremoniously.

I'd like to reemphasize it was just a trim. Even if I had cut my hair poorly it's unlikely I would have noticed a significant change.

But change doesn't come in the time it takes to snip a pair of scissors.

A trim doesn't miraculously heal your hair. A trim every month, proper nutrition, proper handling and most importantly, time, however, does.

This lesson is easily learned when pertaining to my hair because, quite frankly, I didn't care that much about it.

It's the things you care about that are so difficult to have patience for. It's the things that keep you up at night crying because you wish you were better that are harder to accept and work past.

I'm an artist. More specifically I'm a Visual Development artist. I have the responsibility to create, represent, and translate ideas and capture them for film and animation. This trade and my techniques didn't come easily. I had my fair share of doubts and concerns. Fortunately, I've had the privilege of working and learning with some amazing individuals. Surprisingly, the best lessons I've received had little to do with artistic technique and everything to do with life.

"Do the best you can do right now." It was all too easy to surround myself by masters of my craft and compare myself to them. They were better than me.

They were faster than me. Perhaps they were, perhaps they weren't. But they too had likely hurdled their fair share of inner demons.

I don't think it's a uniquely artistic trait to compare ourselves to others, most Members of the 21st century can probably relate to comparing ourselves to magazine images or coworkers, but we do so to our own detriment.

For me, it was just about every artist I saw in my favorite "Art of" books. I admired their shape design and their line-work. None of my work looked like theirs. In retrospect, that's a good thing! I began improving when I studied the things I liked about my favorite artists and made my own interpretation using those skills. Sometimes that's easier said than done.

Point is I couldn't be them if I tried. I wasn't born when they were, I wasn't born where they were, and even if I went to the same school and used the same supplies they did, I didn't go through the same life choices they did. Instead, I made my own decisions and found my own inspirations. We're made up of all our experiences, and those experiences shape the story we have to tell and the interpretation we make of it. It's important to remember everyone's experience is valid. I'm the only one who could tell the stories in my head because I was the only one who had them! The person who could best draw my vision was me. I just had to allow myself to practice. I had to stop comparing and start learning. WHY did I like their work? What was making their images so appealing?

I had to accept where I was, and to do that, the only person I could compare myself to was myself!

For that very purpose, I keep some old drawings available to cringe at. I say available to cringe at because really they're so awful that they cause physical pain to look at!! But realistically, I'm pretty proud of how bad they are. I only recognize those mistakes because I've grown so much as an artist. I didn't see those mistakes when I first drew them.

One of the other things I like to remind myself of is to Kiss. No...Really! K.i.s.s. translates to Keep it simple stupid!

Sometimes, I get caught up in all of the lessons I've learned. There is a lot of data corrugating in my mind and it bumbles with each new project. I used to find myself wanting to keep a checklist just to make a sketch. Light on dark, remember value, remember the rule of thirds, don't forget about you're line weight, flat against curves, the patella faces the same direction as the foot, etc etc. KISS is something to remember at times like these. I reduce my ideas to the basics. What am I trying to say with this drawing? I focus on making sure that my actions translate that. For example, if it's a sad character, I let that emotion dictate where I bring my pencil- into the posture, the coloring, the detailing. I want everything to translate the idea that he's sad. When I reduce some of the chatter in my head, I let myself absorb the lessons I've learned and, I naturally use them. I just have them focused on a singular goal, so it's easier to just let it come naturally.

One of my favorite lessons I've collected is "Slow is smooth, smooth is fast." I have watched many an artist flick their hands across the page, and BAM just like that there's a masterpiece! Or at least that's what it seemed like. They made it look so effortless. In reality they weren't fast; they were efficient. They allowed themselves the time to learn. Precision and speed come from practice. I saw the final image, not the years of sketching, schooling, and experience.

If you want to get good at something, you have to work at it. You can bet that they slowed down to get that fast. They slowed down, they kept it simple, and they reminded themselves that the only way they'll get better is if they let themselves get better.

Despite all of this, at times I have doubted myself, and I thought perhaps I wasn't good enough. It just wasn't in my blood. But here I am today, because I couldn't have ever stopped drawing. I spend sleepless nights thinking about my drawings because I am passionate about it. I firmly believe that with passion, anything is possible. You can always learn to improve, you can always learn as long as you let yourself improve.
You will make mistakes, and you will swear you'll never do it again, but if you really want something, you get back up on that horse, and you do it again and again until you've done it right. Experience is the fastest path to success.

We are magicians in our universe. We have the power to start over whenever we want to and make ourselves the people we wish to be. But we have to let ourselves get there. Patience is a virtue, they say, and nothing could be further from the truth.

KRISTI BAXTER

In today's world I believe we all will have multiple careers, some say 2-4 others say more than that. I never would have thought when I started my career that I would be where I am today, and it makes me wonder what's waiting around the corner.

For as long as I can remember I loved marketing and advertising. As a child of the '70's and '80's when a new product came out, one usually heard about it on TV. Thankfully my mom loved to try new things and happily purchased the newest, greatest things. I also had nearly every popular ad jingle committed to memory and can probably still sing many of them today (although I don't think anyone would want to hear that). I knew from an early age that marketing and possibly advertising were where I would start my career.

Always being one to aim high, I targeted The Walt Disney Company after graduating from college and landed a marketing job with them in Consumer Products. Disney was a fabulous training ground and an amazing place to work. 20+ years later I still look back on my experience there with fondness and appreciation. It was a fun, fast-paced learning environment and I got to work with smart, wonderful people. I reached a ceiling there as I didn't have an MBA, so I went back to business school where I met my husband.

After business school I continued my marketing career in brand management at The Coca-Cola Company. It was another wonderful work experience where I had the opportunity to learn traditional brand marketing from one of the best companies. While I was at Coke, our group hired a coach to resolve some leadership and personnel issues. His job seemed really cool and the seeds of something new were planted- I wanted to do what he did!

A job change for my husband brought us to the Boston area which is not the hotbed of big marketing organizations. I wasn't in a rush to find a job either as we were starting a family. For the first time in my life I had to think about what else other than marketing I would like to do? This was tough because not only did I like marketing, I was good at it. I felt as if I was walking away from something I loved and excelled at and the years of work I'd put in wouldn't necessarily be valued in a different function or industry.

I serendipitously ended up recruiting for a company owned by a longtime family friend. It was a great opportunity to learn new skills and work from home as I was now a new mom. I liked some components of recruiting, but others I found frustrating. I didn't have the passion for it that I did for marketing. What I most enjoyed was interacting with the candidates; what motivated them, what were their leadership experiences like, what did they learn in their professional journey, what did they really want to do next? I also loved interviewing people.

I knew recruiting wasn't the end all be all for me, so again I started thinking about what was next. For someone who was always so directed and knew what I wanted to do, I found not knowing extremely uncomfortable and unsettling. As is usually the case, God knows when I need to hear something even if I don't know what it is. I had a conversation with someone who said, just relax and stop thinking about it so much, the answer is there but you have be ready to listen for it. Sage words. Not long after I was speaking with a candidate who said I would make a great coach. I immediately thought back to the coach at Coke and the pieces fell into place.

I pursued my coaching education and once again was ready for another career pivot, starting over once again this time on my own. This for me was one of the scarier parts as I'd always worked for someone else. Being totally on my own was not easy and figuring out how to run my own business created a new set of challenges. I was great at marketing products, but marketing myself was a horse of a different color. This is still a developmental opportunity for me that I continue to work on.

At the same time I started coaching, I was approached by someone about being a co-host on a couple of local radio shows. I had the opportunity to interview many interesting business people, thought leaders and experts in the areas of small business, leadership, talent management and all things related to the people side of business. I learned more in a few years of interviewing people than I probably could in 10 years of studying business. What started as something that seemed like fun to try ended up being one of the better learning experiences I've had.

I often ask people what advice would you give your 20-something self. If I were going back I would definitely tell myself to think about a career that's flexible. It's much easier today than when I started out in the '90's, but flexibility is really important. I also would say be open to anything that comes your way, even if you didn't expect it. Many successful people will tell you there is a bit of luck involved and being it the right place at the right time, but after interviewing many of them, I realize they kept their eyes open to new opportunities and possibilities. I'd also tell myself if something seems interesting learn about it, pursue it, and see if it's a passion. I wonder where I would be now if I'd done that with the coach at Coke.

One key lesson which I think comes with age is not to be defined by what you do or who you work for. When I worked for Disney and Coke, I loved telling people about what I did and because of the brand recognition, most people loved hearing about it. I've learned that no matter what you do, the most important thing is who you are. I've also learned that each chapter, whether professional or personal is building to something else. Working for Disney and Coke has opened a lot of doors for me over the years, recruiting taught me the art of interviewing and listening, two skills I use frequently today. As I continue with my career, I know there will be other new starts and pivots that I can't yet imagine. One thing I'm always cognizant of is we can't connect the dots when we look forward, only when we look backwards. I can't wait to see what dots fall into place next.

LYDIA ELLE

Everyone thought I was crazy. If I were to be honest, by the time I heard all of their hesitations I almost began to wonder the same thing. Who was I to think that this could work? Who was I to think that I deserved to live the full life I chose instead of the one life tradition had chosen for me? 'You're divorced.' They said. 'You're a single mom,' they jived. 'Are you sure?' It wasn't long before the verses of their questions became the chorus of my own, but I knew within me that the power I had to change the song would be awesome if I chose to keep on singing it, above the questions, above the seeming uncertainty, above the noise. If I listened to the silence of the peace that came when I made the decision, I would be able to maintain it.

I was 35 and moving from the east coast to LA to go into the entertainment industry. I was leaving a very cushy job with the Department of Defense, selling everything I owned and going for my own dreams. And I was taking my 5-year-old daughter with me.

Yes, I know, it sounds crazy…to leave 'stability' on the outside, for peace on the inside. To leave assured income trickling in, to try for an overflow pouring in because of my abilities. But I just *had* to do it and I felt that if I didn't do it now, I would never do it, that I would wonder for the rest of my life if I could do it. If I didn't do it now, I would never show my daughter the most important lesson that I want to teach her which is this. I don't want you to be like mommy, I want you to be like you. If you are the you-est you that you can be because I'm the me-est me, then you will make mommy most proud.

I gave in my notice in March, believing that I shouldn't wait until closer to my moving time to do so. Although I was not leaving D.C. until June, I wanted to allow for enough notice on the projects I needed to complete, but also because I believe God wanted to know how committed I was. Delaying the notice, would delay my commitment to the decision… would delay my commitment to myself. And that was all a part of this process. Carrie Fisher says it best ' do it even if it scares you.' I was certainly scared, but I knew I had to do it.

I sold everything I had. When I got divorced 5 years earlier, I had moved all of my furniture from my house in the south to D.C. So a lot of the story was still replaying as I held on to what was a part of that past. Once I decided to move across the country though, I knew that it was to be the ultimate new beginning. I knew that there needed to be room for the new which meant I had to get rid of the old. I held on to a lot of those things out of fear. I did not know exactly how I would replace them, but I needed to trust this decision in knowing that it would happen. Selling all of my things and putting just the essentials I had in my new car (I replaced my 25 year old car with a new one just before I left) and shipping it across the country was what was supposed to happen. The down sizing process was great. With every item I asked myself 'Lydia, do you really need this?' I learned here that I could survive on so little, that much of what I had was cluttering, not just my space, but my mind. It had to go.

I arrived in LA in February and, after a brief stint searching for a place while staying with a dear friend, I found the perfect spot for my daughter and I's new beginning. The amazing thing is that this spot was a house. A fully detached house! This spot was in a gated community so she would be safe playing AND this spot was FULLY furnished. This means that if I had brought all of my furniture from DC, if I hadn't of listened to the 'yes' within me instead of the no glaring without, I wouldn't have had any room for it. I was overwhelmed with such joy when I found it and the landlord said 'I believe in your vision' when he decided to lease it to me over some more 'stable' applicants. Just before I moved I wrote the manuscript to my first book. When it was finally released in November of 2016 it became a best seller in 6 hours!!!!! I made room for the unknown, knowing that it would work out. I knew that starting over here, meant ending something else there, but it was necessary. My story was not to be confined to that chapter. This is the beginning of my new one with many more to come.

Instagram, Twitter: @iamLydiaElle
Facebook: Lydia Elle
LinkedIn: Lydia Elle

Mindset & Business Consultant
International Speaker
Best Selling Author

LYNNE BRYAN PHIPPS

I'll never forget the night.
It was late, and I was sitting on the sofa with my husband having ice cream and watching the news when the phone rang.
The silence on the other end was long and lasting.
It was my father. He didn't call often, and this call was certainly the most difficult one I think he ever had to make. I don't say this lightly – my father is a surgeon, and he made many many difficult calls in his life.

His voice was silent and when he spoke the pain in his voice was palpable.
Kathy is dead he said…
I screamed….
I ran around the room.
I screamed so loud and so long…..
I then I too was silent.

What?
How?
So many questions, and no answers. Not yet.

That night…. The next day….. the next month and year for that matter were a blur.
What does it mean when you're 28 and your 26 year old sister with so much life and talent and so much to live for dies suddenly and violently? How do you understand it? Where do you put such information in the framework of life?

I remember describing the experience this way; it was like the world went from Technicolor to black and white in one night. I was pregnant with my second child, and all I could think of was that I didn't want this to affect my baby. I had already lost other children before their births. Those losses had sent me on a quest to understand. I was in my 3rd year of Seminary when Kathy died and now I was asking more questions. How does this happen? What does it mean when you realize that if it could happen to your sister it could certainly happen to any of us.

At first, I couldn't get out of my own way. I wandered around thinking about

the reality of parallel universes.
How could everyone else go on living? Didn't they know that everything had changed? Why didn't they get the memo?

I started over. I started seeing everything differently.

I realized that whatever it was that I was living, this thing we call life, was the only chance I had. And if I didn't get on with living, I wouldn't be able to blame anyone but myself. While at the same time I knew I had to become whatever I needed to be and do whatever I needed to do, I also realized that I didn't have any idea what that was.

What I did know is that there were lots of things it wasn't.
I began to realize my own power and to take it back.
Now that sounds easy, but it really isn't, because most of us give our power away and don't even realize we did it.
When we listen to what others tell us what we "should" or "shouldn't" do or want, we give our lives away to others.
When we let negative self talk tell us we "can't" or "won't",
We give away any possibility that we can or could.
When we tell ourselves we will do something tomorrow, or when the kids grow up, or when we retire, we postpone our own lives; and who knows how long we will have or whether we will ever get around to whatever it is that we are dreaming or imagining.

Please be assured - I wouldn't wish anything like what my family and I have experienced on anyone.
And
I want to say that eventually, I learned a skill that I call shifting perspective.
I call it a skill because it takes practice, and intention.

When you shift perspective, you become aware of different ways of understanding the world around you, people around you, or even experiences that you have. When you shift perspective it happens because you think differently.

When I shifted my perspective, I began to make decisions differently....
I rethought things like privilege, expectations, beliefs, roles, and many more concepts. I began to grow into the person I was becoming, and I left behind

the person that I thought others wanted me to be. Notice – I said the person "I thought" others wanted me to be…. Because it really comes down to one thing….

Each of us is our own person, with our own way of being in the world….

Each one of us is perfect in our own imperfection. Magnificently created, we are the only one who can be our own expression in the world.

That's a pretty amazing opportunity. I decided I wanted to take that amazing opportunity, and become my"Self." Almost 30 years later, I can tell you, I'm so glad I did.

Www.inspiritedliving.com
Www.beachwoodri.org
Twitter - Inspirited life
Instagram - Inspirited life
FB - Beachwood RI
FB - Inspirited living

MARY THOMAS PICKETT

See you at the finish line.

A year ago, I became viral from a post I made about a writing professor in college who told me I would never find a career in the magazine industry. Over 10,000 people on LinkedIn resonated with the new "Stick It to The Man" post on their news feed as I celebrated becoming the editor of a magazine at 25 years old.

This goes out to the writing teacher in college who told me I'd never find a career in the magazine industry. 3 months of around the clock work ends with Contributing Editor under my name on that bright shiny mast head in the greatest book of the decade #FacesoftheSouth #livingmydream

Here I was, listening to a street performer below me playing a lovely flute melody, realizing I was a living testament of sorts. Here was real proof that you can start from the bottom and make it wherever you want. I was only 25, sitting in my office in downtown Savannah overlooking historic Wright Square, editing copy that would soon be published in the next issue of *South* Magazine.

That night, after retreating back to my waterfront home that I was able to afford on the Wilmington River, I wiped away tears of joy and disbelief. Just one year before, I was sitting with a counselor discussing my terrible withdrawals from a gnarly benzo addiction. *"I really can do anything,"* I thought to myself, watching the summer sunset from my dock.

When I was hooked on klonopin at 24 years old, I wanted to blame the doctor who had carelessly prescribed me three of the pills a day, "as needed". I was given 90 pills that I abused each month for almost a year. At some point amongst waking up in an ambulance on Bourbon St, looking in the mirror with two black eyes, to rushing for the bathroom at work, to vomit through my withdrawals–I recognized a daunting truth, and the first of many life lessons. **I am in charge of my body, where it goes and what happens to it.**

Through this major life change, I learned a valuable set of important life lessons that with time, have separated me from the rest of my peers stuck in their 20-something limbos. The second lesson I learned can be expressed through a quote by Robert Burns, "Now's the day, and now's the hour." **It's never too late to change where you're at in life. Just do it. Now!**

At that time, I was living in my friend's parents' pool house because my parents wanted nothing to do with my reckless benzo-controlled behavior. Despite my estrangement, I had clothes on my back and a soft bed to sleep in every night. For some folks, this is more than enough. For me, it was not even close to what I knew I was capable of. One day out of the blue, I took a leap of faith and applied for a job with the magazine that I had always dreamed of working for.

When you start doing things out of your comfort zone, the universe will reward you. I woke up the morning of my interview and realized my phone had been stolen at a party over the weekend. Though I had landed the interview and was very hopeful for the job, I still had not gotten serious about the expectations I had for myself. How would I be able to find the office in Savannah without a phone or navigation system? I almost decided not to go. I luckily had a friend look me firmly in the eye and say, "You're going. You will figure it out."

On the way to my interview, I passed a small Verizon store in a Winn Dixie shopping complex in a little town I was passing through. I stopped and purchased my own phone plan, setting me back $700 but navigating me to my interview right on time. **If you have nothing to lose, nothing can stop you - so go for it.** This is not an idea that originated on my own. It took a lot of people telling me this in many different versions before it sunk in. Scraping up the money to afford a U-Haul, rent deposit, and finding the resourceful courage to steal old cardboard boxes from the dumpster behind Family Dollar was all my own doing but it wasn't without the encouragement of others. You can't swing a major life change all on your own. **You have to humbly accept the help you're given – however it's given.**

For almost two years, I used those stolen cardboard boxes that I had taped back together as nightstands and a vanity. I regretfully declined many exciting lunch and dinner invitations to eat PB&Js on my favorite bench in Wright Square. My office was more comfortable and much safer than the room I was renting, so I would stay there every night until almost 8 PM. I would leave the office and complete my daily training for the upcoming half marathon I had signed up for. **I didn't like every sacrifice I had to make, but I liked who I was becoming.**

Those sacrifices had gotten me farther than I had ever imagined. Before long, I was a guest starring on a reality television show, speaking on podcasts, running a charity organization for a philanthropic athlete in the College Football Hall of Fame, even talking to large groups of students about my tips to make it in the magazine industry. Eventually I had my own team of interns who would willingly complete tasks for me and looked to me as a mentor and role model.

At that point, I became overzealous with confidence and started to lose touch of the life lessons I had instilled in myself during those long first months on my journey. Everyone congratulated me because I had worked so hard and come so far. In my mind, it seemed like I deserved some sort of a break. Wasn't it supposed to get easy now? **The next life lesson was learned through the profound words of the rapper, Lil Wayne, "Don't [you] ever get too comfortable."**

I had reached a false comfort level in life that much compared to the way I'd felt back when I took the benzos. I reverted back to having an exaggerated sense of entitlement that exposed some of my not-so ethical choices at work and in my personal life. In January, I decided to resign from my position at *South* magazine to do some inward thinking. I made the decision so quickly that as soon as it happened, I felt an immense amount of regret. Why did I make such a mistake? The answer to this question was found when I stumbled upon a quote by Robert Bach. **"There are no mistakes. The events we bring upon ourselves, no matter how unpleasant, are necessary in order to learn what we need to learn; whatever steps we take, they're necessary to reach to places we've chosen to go."**

Here I am today, on the path to another life change. Currently unemployed and recently evicted, sometimes I wake up feeling like there is a pound of bricks on my chest. I have to remind myself every morning, *"Relax."* **We can easily fool ourselves by thinking we are being proactive by agonizing over dilemmas. We have to trust that a new change, a new start, is just around the corner and still have dreams.**

I don't need to compete or seek validation from anyone to know my dreams are of any worth. Plus, I have a good heart. Despite a gruesome eviction, I have still a roof over my head because others love and care for me. For that I am so grateful! I wish others well and I strive to be better myself. This is my journey – no one else's.

MELINDA COX HALL

Starting over is something that never crossed our minds after 37 years of marriage, but on December 11, 2013 everything we thought was so important completely disappeared, never to be thought of again. The Lord brought all our lives to a screeching halt and sent us on an unexpected journey that dropped us to our knees in a test of Faith unlike anything we have ever faced before, and it changed our lives forever.

I was babysitting our grandchildren when I got a call from the hospital. The nurse asked if I was Melinda Hall. I replied with a frantic "Yes." She said "Your son, John Wright was brought to ER, and he is being admitted to ICU. Get here as soon as possible." I had no idea what happened to him. I called my husband, Craig, our daughter, and our other two sons, and told them to rush to the hospital. When I arrived, I was not expecting what I saw. John Wright was a young, healthy, 33 year old who became an engineer for BNSF Railroad in August of 2013, his dream job. He had just taken a train from Memphis to Pine Bluff, Arkansas the night before. My brain could not comprehend what I was seeing. I could hear a frightening noise, and when I looked into his room, I saw he was on Life Support. My knees nearly buckled. A doctor walked over to us, shaking his head and said "I don't think he's going to make it". I cannot describe the anger I felt. We had just arrived at the hospital. I said "He just got here, and you're already giving up??" At that moment, the Chaplain walked over and introduced himself. His presence meant death, and I did not want to see him. He assured me he was only there for comfort, nothing more, but I wanted him to go away. I have never experienced anything so helpless and gut-wrenching in my entire life. Every parent's worst nightmare was unfolding before our very eyes, and we had no control over any of it. John Wright was lively, funny, healthy, and happy. He had more friends than we ever knew.

As word got around, the ICU waiting room began to fill and overflow into the hallways. There were so many people, the hospital asked them to leave. I began to keep people updated on Facebook so they could hear updates on John Wright's condition straight from his mother with no chance for rumors.

We kept vigil for four long days and nights. We slept in chairs, wearing the same clothes we arrived in. We couldn't leave him. I left only to go to the chapel where I got on my knees beneath the cross and prayed like I have never prayed before. I begged God to take me instead and to heal my child. I have never begged and cried so hard in my life. At 2:30 pm on December 15, 2013, God answered my prayer, in His own way. We gathered around John Wright's bed and after the 5th code blue over four days, I looked up at the nurse and said, "turn it off". I had never heard anything so horrible, so silent, so still. We had lived with that sound for days, almost a sound of comfort because it meant he was still with us.

We left his room after holding him one more time, and walked back through an empty waiting room that was eerily quiet, filled with random pillows, blankets, coats, food, and lost hope. It had been our home for days. Craig and I held onto each other as we walked down the hospital hallways one last time. They were lined with weeping people on both sides of us making phone calls. I heard one after another say "he didn't make it" - "he's gone". John Wright, our wild child, had died. We were numb. As we walked out of the hospital without him, wondering how we would survive the horror we had just lived through, I felt the fresh winter air hit my face. At that moment, I saw the faces of the Sullivan brothers..."all five". Mr. & Mrs. Sullivan had lost five sons at once during WW2. I knew, at that moment, I would survive.

John Wright's funeral drew crowds like we have never seen here before… rich, poor, young, and old, and every one of them said "John Wright was my best friend." He was nice to everyone whether he liked them or not. "Keep your friends close, your enemies closer", he'd say. I found myself comforting hundreds of people without shedding a tear because they had lost their "best friend". I couldn't cry. I was afraid if I ever started, I would never stop. We were in shock. Shock is a wonderful thing. It protected us from the horror we had been through. I have told many grieving people, "I know where you are. Stay there as long as possible." Sometimes I think we are still in that place.

As the days, weeks, and months went by, we had to handle his affairs. It was technical, no time for emotion, a necessary evil. I remember calling AT&T to turn off his phone. The agent said John Wright had his remaining contract to fulfill. My response was, "He died." Silence. The agent put me on hold, and when she came back, I could tell she was deeply affected. She waived all fees, told me to keep the phone, and expressed her deepest condolences, no death certificate necessary. It was an unexpected random act of kindness.

My husband of over 40 years, Craig Hall, is an attorney, and we had a new estate to open, but not just any estate....John Wright's estate, and this one had to be perfect. I have typed many petitions and orders to open estates, so I thought this one wouldn't be any different. I began to type "In Re: The Estate of John Wright Hall, deceased", and it sucked the breath right out of me. We wanted to take care of everything ourselves, but it was an overwhelming task we had in front of us.

I have been on social media for years and for different reasons, mainly to support America's heroes. I did not need a job, so I let my LinkedIn account sit until I could figure out what to do with it. I began posting support, appreciation, and inspiration for our heroes. Little by little, it started catching on, and the responses were, and continue to be, very positive and filled with gratitude. I have had people reach out to me because they feel my compassion, many with PTSD, none of them knowing my story. I am not a professional, so I am extremely careful with my words. I respond to them without thought. Words flow effortlessly through my fingers from somewhere deep in my soul that could only come from Angels or Almighty God. I have re-read messages I have sent to these starving souls, and I do not remember any of it. The words are always comforting, even to me when I re-read them. This was a gift from God that I would not have had He not taken John Wright. I live my life to touch the hearts and lift the spirits of others who cross my path. As painful as his death was, other parents have suffered much worse, some never knowing what happened to their children. John Wright was a man of great Faith. He is not missing. I know exactly where he is, and he has seen the face of Jesus. It does not get any better than that. I would not bring him back here for anything. He finished his job here on earth early. For us, there was life before he died, and life after he died. They are two completely different lives.

I chose to support and thank our Military and First Responders because they need it badly. My passion comes from the unbearable pain in my heart. I consider this pain a gift. I am still standing because I refuse to wallow in self-pity and grief. God gave me a test I never thought I could survive.... ever. No parent does. I intend to pass this test and touch as many lives as I can until I see John Wright again. I never ask "why". I am humbled God chose a child we raised for His work. Many grieving parents have said to me, "Why my son? I want him back!" God gave His Son for me, so why not my son? God expects us to lean on Him in good times and in bad. He will never abandon us. I am grateful to God for the gift He has given me. Without this tremendous loss, I would not have the compassion and the vision needed to help others.

The wallpaper on John Wright's iPhone was 1 John 1:5 "God is Light; In Him there is no darkness at all." That verse is also inscribed on his tombstone. If we always look to the Lord, He will light the way. I never take my eyes off Almighty God. I pray daily for all who need peace and comfort. 'Blind Faith' gets me through the darkness. I hold the lantern to show others the way. God shines His light in the lantern I carry for Him.

LinkedIn: linkedin.com/melindahall us

Twitter:
@melindacoxhall
@Sept11Memorials

Facebook:
www.facebook.com/melindacoxhall/
www.facebook.com/oldcollierville/

Instagram:
@peerintothepast

Pinterest:
www.pinterest.com/peerintothepast/

"In tribute to Mrs. Sullivan and her five sons"

Michelle Dunton

I WAS MY MOM'S BEST FRIEND

Those six words sums up our relationship. When you are someone's best friend, it is a huge responsibility. And, that's exactly what it was. Being her best friend was a HUGE responsibility.

The last words she said to me before she died were "I love you more." I had just told her that I loved her. That may not seem like a big deal these days, but those words were just never spoken in my house — not by her, not by anybody. It was implied. I show up everyday, therefore, I love you.

I remember the exact moment I found out about her cancer. She sent it to me in a text. I was walking to the kitchen, my phone buzzed and I opened it up. Her words were, "Well, I definitely have pancreatic cancer." The day was September 17, 2011.

I wish I could say I was shocked. Unfortunately, she had just been in the hospital for pancreatitis. It only seems natural that pancreatic cancer was not too far away. But, when they dismissed her just two weeks before her visit to the doctor, they told her there was not one trace of cancer in her body.

Thus, began my huge dislike for the medical community. How could they reassure her like that and then send her for more tests only to find out she did indeed have cancer??

But, here's the thing, not just cancer, stage 4 pancreatic and lung cancer.

So, there I was at 47 years old, finding out my mom was going to die at 64. I knew there was no hope, I just didn't know on that day how little time I had left — it was less than 2 months.

Looking back, I'm happy I didn't know. I think God gives us these things as we are able to handle them. Even after knowing about her cancer, I wasn't freaking out yet. I'm sure some people would say it was denial. I really don't think it was. In 1988, my dad had died of pancreatic cancer. I had very little recollection as to what he went through, but I was fully aware that stage 4 pancreatic cancer meant no cure.

As you can see, my mom and I were only 17 years apart. She was married and had me before her high school graduation. She had to quit school, get married and have a baby while most girls her age were enjoying their senior year.

We fought like sisters. We took turns being the mom. And, through her cancer, we discovered how to tell each other that after it was all said and done we could say those words. They had never been spoken before.

I spent almost the entire last 7 weeks of her life with her. I did for her the things she did for me as a child. I bathed her. I put make up on her. I brushed her hair. I yelled at her when she wouldn't take her medicine. I fed her. I screamed at nurses and doctors. And, when she was sleeping and didn't see me, I sat next to her and cried, like I'm sure she did many times in my life.

I have never had to be so strong as I was when she was in the hospital. I hate hospitals, like most people, and I never thought I could spend so many hours in a hospital.

Watching her disappear, that's what she did, from cancer, made me hate the word. I wish I could say that cancer brought us closer together, but that truly wasn't possible.

I talked to my mom every day of my life until November 5, 2011. Sure, there were times we fought, more times than not during some years. But, whether I talked to her on the phone, in person or in my head, she was the only constant in my life.

I am grateful that cancer took her as quickly as it did. She didn't have to deal with chemotherapy or radiation. I'm not sure she would have handled it well. They did offer it to her, which is unbelievable given her diagnosis, but she gave the paper to me and said, "Tell them no." And that's what I did. I said no to putting her through more pain than she was already in. I had to say the word "no" a lot during that time.

"No, Mom, you can't walk. Your legs don't work anymore."

"No, Mom, I know you're thirsty, but you can't drink anything."

"No, Mom, I know you are in pain, but I can't give you any more medicine."

I still have nightmares about having to say no to her. All she wanted to do was walk, drink something and be out of pain. I couldn't give her those things. I used to pray she would understand on some level I wasn't trying to torture her, I was trying to help her.

The absolute best thing I learned from my mom's cancer was that death was only an illusion. I don't know anyone who was more afraid to die than she was, but when she knew it was inevitable, she helped me see what she was seeing.

It was the Tuesday before she died. Her and I were alone in my dining room, which was now her room since we could fit the hospital bed in it, she looked at me and said, "Tell your dad I'm not going with him tonight." I said, "Mom, Dad isn't here. I can't talk to him." She looked right at me in shock and said, "He is standing right next to you. I've already told him before and he won't go away." I have to say at that moment, I was a little freaked out. I've read about people who are really sick seeing loved ones who have already passed away, but this wasn't just seeing him. She was actually talking to him and could see him standing right next to me.

Then, later that night she said to me, "Who is the woman in the red coat that keeps coming into your house?" I said, "Mom, no one is here but us." She said, "No. There is a woman in a red coat who keeps wandering around your house. She sometimes comes in and smiles at me." Even after she passed away, I always thought about who that woman was.

I learned death is not final. She saw my dad. She was not hallucinating. She was as clear as I was. There is a forever.

How did I start over?

It wasn't easy. I'm not going to lie. I let myself go through the numbness before I actually sat down and thought about what my mom went through. It did not happen at once. As a matter of fact, I was probably numb the whole first year. But, by the second year, I started to gain some perspective. And, since it has now been five years, I am able to write about what she taught me with a hint of sadness and lots of sweetness.

She taught me to not be afraid to die. She was afraid of dying up until she died. One day, like a day or two before she passed away, she looked at me and said, "I think I have MS because I can't move my hands right. Please tell the doctors." I thought it was so sad. I wanted to say, "Mom, what you have is a whole lot worse than MS." But, even though she was dying, the fear of dying didn't leave her.

I learned that no matter how afraid of dying you are, it doesn't matter - you are still going to die. You can not force yourself to live by spending your life being afraid to die.

She taught me to be happy every day. Her motto before she became ill was to be content with life. She always said I shouldn't expect happiness. But, one day, one of her last days, she looked at me and said, "Be happy no matter what. I wish I would have chose happiness."

She taught me to say "I love you" every day and as often as you can. I KNOW she loved me. But, I do wish we would have said it more to each other. I also wish I would have said it more to a lot of people who are no longer with me, both living and dead. Showing someone you love them is absolutely necessary. But, words still matter. I now say "I love you" as many times a day as I can.

No one likes the word "cancer." That word has invoked fear for many generations. But, if you choose, you can make it as much of a blessing as it seems to be a curse. It started as a curse back in 1988, but today, I choose to see it as a blessing - because everything is exactly as we see it - and I've lived long enough to know that if I see it as a blessing, then it becomes one.

I was my mom's best friend for 47 years. There was no greater joy.

Facebook - https://www.facebook.com/mmdunton
Linked In - https://www.linkedin.com/in/michelle-dunton-804b2053/
Twitter - https://twitter.com/MichelleDunton
Youtube Channel - Writing Fun - https://www.youtube.com/channel/
UCGea5qQGIQiaxXguujY2KhA

Michelle Rutter

I have known the ups and downs of life, and have had a successful career in freelance writing. I have dealt with career changes and uncertain incomes, all the while working to find a way to provide for my family. My parents divorced when I was eight years old which had a huge effect on my life, thoughts, and well-being. Although, I didn't let the change in lifestyle affect me completely, I soon grew accustomed to living my life in two halves. There have been a number of incidents that have made me sit up and take a look at life and question it.

My mum and dad splitting up wasn't as bad as I can remember as a child, when in 2003 I learned that my nephew, who was only 9 at the time, had cancer. We all know the word and know what it means, but I don't think we truly take in the actual seriousness of it until it happens to someone we love. I'm not a religious person, but I found myself praying that my nephew got through his sickness. I made all kinds of promises to someone I didn't know and couldn't see in return that my nephew lived, and surely after a year and a half of hospital visits, worry and pain, my nephew got through it and is now a healthy, happy, 23 year old.

At the same time my nephew became sick, I became pregnant at the age of 23. I was preparing to have my first child. I was so excited but scared at the same time as I really didn't have a clue what to do. Like all new parents, babies do not come with instruction manuals although if they did, I guess they would have helped, as I tend not to follow instructions very well.

My daughter was due to be born on the 21st of July, 2004. She was two weeks late. I was booked into the hospital to have them start my labour off on the 2nd of August, 2004. As soon as I got to the hospital, I was prepared to be induced and surely that night my labour began. Still, by 12pm on the 3rd of August, I had only dilated by 2cm and was in a lot of pain.

They allowed me to have my gas and air which I had no problem taking. They put another type of liquid into my tube which would apparently speed up the process more and get the baby out quicker. My daughter didn't react to the liquid very well, and her heart began to beat faster than normal. The doctors said I may have to have a C section as labour wasn't going as well as they hoped.

I started to panic and then my dad turned up after finding out what was going on to see if I was ok. The nurse wouldn't allow him into my room because my partner and mum were already in there. Knowing what was going on and that I may be in trouble, I said I wanted my mum to go out and let my dad come in. If anything was going to happen to me, I wanted to be able to see my dad.

They still wouldn't let him in, so I told my partner to go out and tell my dad I was fine, and that I loved him. As soon as he left the room, the machine alarms went off and a lot of doctors came flying into the room. Apparently, my daughter was struggling and she had released a stool inside and that if they didn't perform a c section as soon as possible, then mine and my daughter's life were in trouble.

They were throwing forms in-front of me saying that if anything happened, the hospital would not be responsible. I refused to sign and all the time had my mum screaming at me to sign them. My partner came back in, to shock and horror as he witnessed the distress I was in. The doctor pulled him to one side and told him that if I signed the forms now, he promised that me and our daughter would be safe.

I eventually listened and signed the forms and surely enough, half an hour later our healthy baby girl was born. Children make a big difference to your life anyway, but almost losing my first born and my own life hit me hard. It made me realize that life is too short to have any grudges and bad feelings in the world. As easy as we are giving life, it can be taken away. In both circumstances, I found myself praying in my head that everything would be fine. I made promises that if my daughter came through the labour alive, then I would do my best to give her the life she deserved, to love her unconditionally, and to be by her no matter what. Since then I have had two more children, another girl, who is now nine, and a little boy, who is five.

There are other stories to tell that has happened to me and made me sit up and think about my life and how I can change, but for now, I think I have my life in order, and I'm living it to the fullest. I can with three children following closely behind.

ℕICOLE ℝRAFT

Growing up in France, watching skilled American surfers ride Atlantic waves, gave me the desire to discover California. So in the 90's, when I was 21 years old, I worked hard, saved money and had my best friend's researcher father put an ad in the San Diego newspaper to stay with an American family that summer. A friendly family with four children answered and showed me the nice San Diego area. This was the beginning of starting over.

In their backyard, I was lucky to see colorful hummingbirds and with them I crossed the Mexican border, went to Seaworld, Balboa Park, etc.….They shared their habits and it was a cultural exchange. That summer, I met a Dutch trainer established at the San Louis Rey Downs' training center near Fallbrook, who asked me to come work for him. I hesitated, as I was busy studying and finally accepted almost a year afterwards, as I felt that I couldn't run away from destiny. I worked hard again that summer and flew to America in September. This time it was the San Francisco Bay area, to work at the Bay Meadows racetrack. That was the start of a new adventure, beginning with my numerous work permits, which were so hard to get.

Two years of hardships followed, with horses facing fierce competition, racing all around the San Francisco Bay area, at the different fair tracks, but also in southern California at Santa Anita, Hollywood Park, and Del Mar. Eventually the stable could not make ends meet, the trainer had to give up his dream, and during 6 days, I drove across America to Lexington, Kentucky. There, I farm sat while the owners went on vacation, and rode green horses for $ 5 a ride. Eventually, I got lucky to start working at Calumet's neighboring farm, which sprawled across 1 000 acres. When their broodmare manager left, I got the position and took care of 100 broodmares and their foals. Being responsible for such a nice collection of fabulous thoroughbred racehorses and foaling their foals was a dream come true. The champion mare "Lady's Secret (by triple crown winner Secretariat), formerly trained by D. Wayne Lukas had been bought by the farm's owner for $ 3.8 million. After four years, the farm's owner sold his 500 horses world-wide and asked the team to start over by becoming a boarding facility. Previously a very private nursery, it was a challenge to now open to boarders and find new clients in a highly competitive environment of 740 Bluegrass already well-established farms.

A strong voice inside of me urged (me) to pick up studies again while working, by taking evening classes. So, I earned an Associate degree in Computer Information Systems and left Kentucky to work with a marketing database at Morgan Stanley in Ocala, Florida. After a short time there, I felt the need to go back to France, but the awakening was hard. In order to pay my bills, I had to work at night, caring for about 60 Alzheimer and elderly patients. Americanized, my acquired pioneering spirit couldn't resign to do this all my life, without using my language and computer skills. I worked at night, and afterwards, when I was finished at 7 am in the mornings, I always searched for other positions. Eventually I found a Personal Assistant job in Bordeaux for a start-up company, providing technical equipment for International show jumping riders. After 2 years there, I reluctantly followed a friend to Eastern France, as he had been hired to work in Switzerland.

Again I had to start over, relying only on my knowledge and skills to find a job. I spent numerous hours looking for a position, sending out hundreds of Curriculum Vitaes, and finally worked in the pharmaceutical business for 4 years. The salary was high, but working in an open space with 40 colleagues, on the 13th floor with 6 elevators, in a building overlooking Basel wasn't a match for me.

I packed my belongings and moved back to the south-west of France where I grew up, and it took me 2 long years to find my current position.

Starting over is all about taking risks, working hard, patience, perseverance, and being at the right place at the right time, with the right people.

Values, connections and wisdom will not lead to glory or fame, but nowadays only, simply to find, and keep your job.

This is the simple message the younger generations should keep in mind: work hard, try your best, be kind to others, don't get easily discouraged, but just keep the faith. Look around, enjoy nature's gifts, forget your daily worries for a few minutes, and then give all your energy for the goal you wish to reach.

Think outside the box, be true to yourself, and you will see doors opening for you in life. Don't be scared to start over :-) Take the blinkers off, follow your instinct, transmit all your knowledge to others.

All of that, I learned long ago in America, also thanks to the best teachers I ever had, and one of them prepared us well for the future. He told us that our generation would have at least 9 different jobs on our C.V. and that it was wise to save at least 1 year salary for tough times ahead.

I'm forever thankful to America and its hardworking people, because without that life experience, and work, I would probably not have had the job I appreciate so much today.

I wish to express my gratitude to:
- Eileen for this surprising writing opportunity
- My family, for their unconditional support and values
- My dedicated teachers for transmitting their knowledge and useful advices
- My employers for their trust
- The hardworking people in every country for their pioneering spirit which inspires me daily
- Lara and her International team for the wonderful opportunities to discover new countries and people, as well as the kind highnesses for their vision, dynamism, creativity and sharing spirits

RICHARD MONTGOMERY

Starting Over.

As I thought about the title, *Starting Over*, it dawned on me how many times in my seventy-five years I have actually *started over*. Many of those times were more or less routine and merely required some mental adjustments to pick up and move on. Others weren't so trivial.

I suspect for many breaking up with your high school sweetheart was the very first *starting over* event in your young life. That was certainly the case for me. Frankly, breaking up was not my choice. Her parents forbid her to see me. However, the parent-imposed quarantine only served to intensify my strong feelings for her.

Consequently, when I headed off to the University of Miami I tried to maintain contact. I wrote to her nearly every week. I sent the letters to one of my closest friends who was aware of the circumstances, and lived right across the street from her. I couldn't understand why she didn't respond, or at least acknowledge my letters. I didn't find out until many years later that my friend purposely did not deliver my communications. In the meantime, she had met someone else, and as fate would have it, they got married.

It took me a long time to realize that my love for her had been much greater than her love for me. One thing that particular *starting over* experience did for me was to strengthen my desire to make something of myself. At that time, it was most certainly the driving force behind my quest to succeed in life. My father had reminded me that success is always the best revenge.

For many, *starting over* occurs at various times, some inopportune. Some are caused by physical problems, some by emotional stress, and others are caused by personal choices. In my case, the next greatest challenge came when I was forty-six years old. It was at a time when I was very successful, and in the prime of life. Before I go into the details, it's important to provide some background.

Since I was about seven years old, I had always been fascinated with airplanes. One couldn't fly overhead without me watching it until it was well out of sight. Like many of my peers during the Vietnam War, I joined the Navy and became a Naval Aviator. I got to fly eight different aircraft, made hundreds of carrier landings on numerous Aircraft Carriers, and accumulated over four thousand flight hours in both prop and jet aircraft. I had certainly realized my childhood dream.

As a result of my military performance, I was selected and sent to the Naval Post Graduate School in Monterey, California, where I was awarded a Master's Degree in Aeronautical Engineering. This was just the beginning of many achievements in my Naval career. It also involved numerous positions including several moves – many of which moved us back and forth across country.

With my degree in Aeronautical Engineering and unique skill set, I was one of the only Commanders uniquely qualified to take over the position as a Section Head in the Air Antisubmarine Warfare Division of the Operational Test and Evaluation Force in Norfolk, Virginia. I was certainly on the fast track to a very successful Naval career.

Typically the position as Section Head was limited to two years since fresh fleet operational experience was preferred. However, the Admirals that I worked for kept extending my tour. After nearly five years, I was nominated to be the Executive Assistant to Casper Weinberger who was then the Secretary of Defense. Quite frankly, being nominated doesn't guarantee the position, but I was one of only three Commanders considered. Moreover, the Admiral that I worked for was assured that I would be selected.

The position of Executive Assistant to the Secretary of Defense guaranteed promotion to Captain, and given a successful tour, promotion to Rear Admiral was a near certainty. Unfortunately, the position would require that I be in Washington DC for the next two years.

Cheryl and I had bought a home on a lake in Virginia Beach. Our daughter Casey not only loved the lake, but also the Christian school she had attended from the very first day it opened. She was at an age when girls really need an active father in their lives. Cheryl had done a wonderful job as a mother, but we both knew that she couldn't fill the role of an absentee father.

While I had an amazing career path, it was not an equally amazing path for my family. There was no way I would move my family to Washington DC only to steal away a few hours a week. So I knew that if I took the job, I would have to leave my family in Virginia Beach.

During my career I had made several decisions that had been very difficult. Up until this time, the most difficult was turning down Test Pilot School. Although, I was not one to look back, that had been the toughest decision that I had made. However, it would have resulted in a third move in a two-year period.

As with the Test Pilot School decision, I decided that family was more important to me than career. Consequently, I withdrew my name from consideration and decided it was time to retire. So after twenty years of Naval Service doing something that I loved, I found myself *starting over*.

Fortunately, growing up, I had a father who was always there for me. He would give me great advice, but more importantly, he convinced me that I was capable of doing anything that I set my mind to accomplish. So it was time to *start over* and begin a new life chapter.

Given my background and experience, I had no trouble getting a job. In fact, my first job was with a defense-contracting firm (BDM Corporation) that provided support to the very Command that I had just left. I found myself walking through the same doors and basically doing the same job. The only difference was that I wasn't wearing a uniform. So my transition was fairly routine, until BDM Corporation lost the follow-on contract.

Thus I found myself *starting over* yet again. I was out of work for a very short period of time when I was contacted by another defense contracting firm, Tracor Applied Science. They really wanted me in Washington DC, but I had decided long ago that I was not moving to Washington DC under any circumstances. That is why I retired and gave up my Naval career in the first place.

During all these transitions, it was technically me who was the one *starting over*, BUT it is always the wife who undergoes the greatest challenge – secretly struggling with the unknown, hiding her inner fears, all the while putting on a brave face in order to provide the support her husband needs.

Following retirement, the wife ends up with twice the husband and half the pay, although as a retired Commander with a good job, money was not an issue for us. However, all that was about to change.

In my new job, I worked out of the house. My boss, Dan Turissini, was a young fellow twenty years my junior. He ran a division for Tracor and was always looking for new business opportunities. In the defense contracting business, you, as an employee, must continue to market yourself in order to maintain your employment.

Now that I've laid the background, I can go into the greatest challenge that faced me when I was in the prime of my life. Dan had found an opportunity with the U.S. Coast Guard. Unfortunately, it was at the end of the fiscal year and Tracor didn't have enough funds to support Dan's marketing initiative. One night I called Dan and said that we should start our own company and go after the work ourselves. Initially my suggestion seemed to be out of the question. However, about an hour later, Dan called me back, and a new company was born.

The next night Cheryl asked how my day went. I was reading the newspaper and casually mentioned that I had quit my job. Cheryl had been preparing dinner and finally realized what I had just said.

"You what?" she questioned, not fully believing the casual announcement.

"I quit my job today," I replied matter-of-factly, without putting down the paper.

"You're kidding," she said after a short pause. "You just got a nice raise," she added.

"Don't worry," I said, "Dan and I are starting our own company."

"And you were going to tell me this...when?" she asked, with obvious concern in her voice.

"Tonight. And before you tell me that we're nuts, we already have our first delivery order."

I had always been aware that Cheryl has a very large security bubble. While in the Navy, we had always discussed my opportunities since the decision would involve the two of us along with a major household move. I probably should have told her what I had in mind, but I had a lot of confidence in my own ability, and I didn't want her to worry unnecessarily. Thus, this was the biggest *starting over* event in our marriage … and quite frankly, in my life.

During the first year in business, I only took a little over twelve thousand dollars in salary. The second year wasn't much better. Dan and I had grown the firm to twelve employees when we finally won a large contract with the Naval Air Systems Command.

From that time on we experienced rapid growth. At eighty plus employees, we won a large contract beating out some very strong competition, including AT&T. We were the sole supplier of Digital Certificates to the entire Federal Government. The contract gained the attention of some major players and eventually led to the sale of our company, and a very secure retirement.

One thing that I have learned in my life from *starting over* is to trust God. Sometimes *starting over* happens by choice and other times it's out of your control. Ultimately, having a personal relationship with God is more important than anything else, any career, any success, all the money in the world. If you have a relationship with Him and trust Him with the direction of your life, everything will fall into place, even if it doesn't make sense at the time. It's so important to seek His will for your life. He sees the entire puzzle, while we only see the tiny pieces. Sometimes it's hard to *start over* and trust Him with the outcome, but it's important to gain perspective – His perspective on every situation. We can try to choose our own path, but that path won't even come close to comparing to the amazing path God has planned for us.

God enabled each of us with unique abilities and desires. He can change your heart to align with His perfect plan for you. It's important to always remember, do something that you know and love, and strive to be the very best at whatever you do along the way. *Starting over* can certainly be a daunting venture, but it's an amazing opportunity at a new chapter, a new adventure, a new you. Here's to new beginnings and *starting over*!

Rony Joseph

The Life of a Servant
Redemption

My Story began in South America (Ecuador) were I was born in a small fisherman town. People knew our family. My dad was a doctor married to a nurse (Gloria). He was a very gifted man with his hands. I had a misunderstood childhood full of tears. I still think of the days when my father was dragging me out the court house and leaving with my father. I could not understand why, but time would pass and the memory of my mother (Gloria) started to fade away. I was robbed of the opportunity to love. I came to America as a last option (10/01/1986). I was excited to be here. I was amazed of the people here. A dream come true, but my reality was different. My father had one intention of leaving us here with our Aunt (Ana). I thought he was coming back, but never saw my father again until I received a phone call a few years back from my sister Janick. He passed away, and I cried for weeks angry of the opportunity of telling him how much I hated him for all the abuse I received and a constant battle trying to live up to his expectations. Now I was part of the prince of the air. This is America where the strong survive and the weak perish. A medium does not exist even when things are seen out of control. I always felt a hand watching over me. I felt it time and time again with countless nights walking alone inside the streets of Brockton. Now I understand why even in the middle of my chaos, God was moving things so I could get to Him. I survived the trials of being a gang member (Black Panthers) a run up and down selling drugs. I never thought of myself being a part of a dark world where you became a puppet and lost days without a way out unless your six feet under. My reality was dark. Put yourself in my shoes, close your eyes and imagine running for your life. Nothing seemed real and every night I asked God for a new life. The time to make a decision for my life came to my door steps that night, opening my door, I found ATF searching my apartment. I was put under surveillance for a few months and did not know. I was scared for my life. They were looking for drugs and guns. It was going to be a long night ahead for me. It was a deep feeling inside of me. I was frozen in time. Just thinking about it brings tears to my eyes. A dark road was placed upon me, why, who could tell me where my angels were hidden from me, and a fountain of sorrow was close inside my soul. Sometimes waiting for the night to come along, I would ask myself, where is God? Why put me inside a circle of pain and for me, there was without a way out until one night in the middle of an encounter with drugs, I felt the presence of hope. Suddenly I found the floor and asked God, 'If you really exist, take me away from this dark hole, and I will give you my life". That is how I began to seek Him and to understand that I did not know who I was talking to. My journey began with an encounter which seemed like an illusion. I was downstairs at my house smoking, and I hear voices telling me that I need something stronger. For a second I thought about a solution to my life and how crazy it is, and that I was tired of feeling lost. For the first time, I felt the air of my lungs needing a way out, so I got on my knees and I said," 'God if you really exist, take this addiction away from me and I will give you my life". 09/29/2008 was the beginning of a battle between two worlds. I always was doubting my own understanding. I lost myself on the pain of losing my family (*divorce) 06/12/2012. I could not understand why would God take me away from my family, but He had a different plan for me. I began my walk with God and learning about creation. Where does a man fit on His divine design? I took to enroll in Terika Smith Ministries where I truly learned to see the landscape of the Word of God. I could see God's hand moving around me, molding me, reshaping my heart. I started a DE intoxication of the world and filling my cup with Love and understanding for lost souls through our church LEC. It wasn't easy. People still cannot see the truth of their lives, but we never stop bringing the gospel all around the city of Lawrence. One night God spoke to me telling me my purpose on His kingdom, build 7 churches around the world. So I am on a new journey, praying and giving people a better understanding of life.

SANDRA HOMER

The Christmas tree is lit up in all colors of the rainbow, my house has Christmas spirit pouring out through every door and window, all the presents are wrapped, and my son, Devin, is hardly sleeping - waiting for Santa Claus to appear. Christmas Eve of 2016 is a night that I will never forget, a night when the life I had been living for 38 years would be changed forever. My health, marriage, and career ended as I knew it, and I was forced to start over. It was the last night I lived inside a strong healthy and energetic body. The next morning, Christmas Day 2016, I woke up to a new beginning - starting my life over with one of the most painful chronic illnesses known to man...I had lupus.

I had slept for maybe four hours Christmas Eve, and I was finishing up a straight 36 hours of working - making custom handmade sympathy gifts for the grieving community. In a matter of 2 days my business, Heavensbook Angels, had generated over 40 orders containing 80 bracelets, 20 necklaces and 12 keychains. I worked tirelessly over the last two days, hardly resting and forgetting to eat, so that my customers would have their gifts by Christmas weekend. When I awoke Christmas morning a searing pain was rushing through my hands. A pain that is indescribable, relentless surges of stabbing shooting pain running through my shoulders down to my fingertips. The pain was so intense, so extreme, that I could not even speak. I sat up in my bed and the only thing I could do was cry.

Three months of lab tests, blood tests, cat scans and ultrasounds finally revealed that I had an autoimmune disease. Two months later, the diagnoses was narrowed down further to mixed connective tissue disorder, lupus and inflammatory arthritis. Within weeks I had lost 20 pounds, and I had been put on a medication regime that consisted of 9 pills a day and weekly injections of chemotherapy. Yes, chemotherapy. The pain from my illness is too much to bear, in addition to becoming violently ill and nauseas for two days after my chemo injections.

Since being diagnosed with lupus, I have lost numerous friends, my husband, and my life as I knew it. Everything in my life has changed. My marriage quickly became on the rocks due to the huge change in the family dynamic. I was no longer the wife that could go food shopping, do the laundry, and shuttle the kids around all day. My social life became anything but social. I canceled plans on just about everyone I knew. The people who tried to understand my illness and could tolerate my mood swings based on the amount of pain I was in - became less and less. My business had also begun to suffer. I could no longer make bracelets! I was expected to make 100-500 bracelets per week, and I couldn't even make 10 without being in immense pain.

It was on July 4th weekend of 2016 that I had an epiphany - my life had to start over in order for me to survive and for my son Devin to have the childhood he deserves. I quickly began trying all the new holistic treatments for lupus including, acupuncture, yoga, and even meditation. Nothing help. Medication only softened the intensity of the pain, but it is always there. The only thing that could take my mind off of the pain long enough to function was seeing my son Devin happy and smiling.

It is so hard to slow down in a universe that is constantly speeding up! I know that my mind, body, and soul need to rest. But I have my own company, and hundreds of thousands of followers on social media that depend upon me to help them through their difficult days and customers that need sympathy gifts. My husband of ten years was having an affair, and I have since filed for divorce. I now have sole custody of my son. Why my husband chose to have an affair after ten years of marriage is an irrelevant question. Instead of sticking by my side, through sickness & in health, he chose to run from me, my illness, and life's challenges, and take his version of the easy way out.

This last year of my life has been a whirlwind of confusion, uncertainty, betrayal and pain. The person I was prior to 2016 no longer exists. I have been reborn into a life in which I must wake up every day and fight. I do not have the choice to run from lupus, the chronic pain, and from being a mother. I choose life. I choose to start over. I choose to face life head on. I am a fighter and a warrior and my new beginning starts now. The pages are empty but are waiting to be filled with memories of love, laughter, and years of happiness.

Https://www.facebook.com/heavensbookangels/
Https://www.instagram.com/heavensbookangels/
www.twitter.com/Heavensbooka

I'M SO AWESOME EVEN MY IMMUNE SYSTEM CAN'T GET ENOUGH OF ME!

www.ThisLupieWorld.com

#LUPUSFACT:

80% of people with lupus experience fatigue. It can be debilitating to the point of forcing them to stop working.

lupus.org

STEPHANIE PAPE

"His Mom Strong - Peace by Piece"

I lost the "Ross to my Rachel" on February 28th, 2015. Luke was diagnosed with a rare, very aggressive form of cancer on May 7th, 2014. The day he got diagnosed marked a new beginning for me, for us, one we didn't want. I was 30 when he died and I wasn't with him when he died, I hate saying that. Luke was very sick and the prognosis wasn't great. I was terrified he would die, but he wouldn't, except he did. Never did I allow myself to truly believe Luke would slip away. Things like that didn't happen to us. Even if I had prepared myself for the thought, nothing could have prepared me for the reality. The process of getting ready for Luke's funeral was odd, I hated everything about it. Standing in my walk in, staring at my clothes, I wept. This wasn't supposed to happen, I wasn't supposed to be here, doing what I was doing. I shouldn't have needed a "Luke's funeral outfit". I was still in disbelief.

We had done all we would ever do, we'd said everything we would ever get to say, and I could only think of the words that would never be said or heard. He was gone, we were done and there was nothing I could do to change it. Six years of being my "Mr. Big", and there was no goodbye, not that ours ever stuck anyway, but this time it would, it had to. He wasn't coming back. Where we were, was where we would stay. Apart. Going through the motions, going to his funeral, coming home and sitting with the fact that he was gone, a new beginning, one I didn't want.

My first Facebook post after losing Luke, outside of the thank you for your condolences posts. March, 12th, I had stumbled upon this quote, "*In the end, I am the only one who can give my children a happy mother who loves life.*" – Janene Wolsey Baadsgaard' A new beginning. It was a wakeup call for me. Did I have a right to be sad? Of course, but my son, J, still needed me, a happy me, regardless of our circumstances. He gets one childhood, I get one shot at being his mom, the kind of mom I want him to remember, a mom who took time to do fun things. I can't and won't waste that opportunity, not for anything. My light was so dim when I posted that quote but J and I still went to his soccer game. I cheered my heart out, we were silly on the way home and we celebrated their win with ice cream (way past his bedtime). A new beginning. A new "normal".

Was I able to put down my grief and be Super Mom every single day after that? No! I've built what I thought was peace more times than I care to count, only to have it torn down by something trivial, I'm talking completely unglued over the smallest inconvenience. That's a harsh realization, that you're farther away than you thought from peace. You take a step forward only to be slammed a few steps back. I didn't realize grief could look so much like anger but I was furious. I journaled my way through grief and if I was anything other than angry, I was inconsistent! What would bring me peace, feel like "a new beginning" one day, would make me angry or sad the next. I couldn't get to the bottom of my grief. I had what I thought were hundreds of "new beginnings" only to realize they were simply steps, baby steps.

The one-year anniversary of Luke's passing was like starting my grief all over again and for some reason it was intensified. I hated February! The entire month reminded me of his pain, reminded me I wasn't there when he passed, reminded me he was gone. Life was going on without him and I hated it! He was gone and after a year, I knew better what that meant and again how much I hated it. Loving someone, losing them and then being forced back into life with the expectation to somehow be happy is still an idea I struggle with. I just don't like it. That first February, without Luke, watched me crumble. Surviving the hell that month was, the hell I made it, getting through the first year, through that month that tried to break me, was a new beginning.

The second-year I didn't lose myself to the month. I gave myself permission to lean into my grief when I needed to. I didn't mistake my tears for weakness, they served as reminders that I had survived two years of February's destruction. I wasn't giving this February another ounce of me. I worked hard to forgive the month and I think maybe I have. A new beginning.

What made the second year so different? While February 28th was my worst day, it was someone else's best day…their birthday, or wedding anniversary. The day will always ache for me but that realization forced me to look at the bigger picture. This life is bigger than me, bigger than Luke. Even the day he was diagnosed, I wanted to hate that day but it is my sister's birthday. How could I hate that day? She's been with me for all my new beginnings. I'm starting to understand why the world must keep moving even when I want it to stop. Good things happen even when bad things happen. That realization was a new beginning.

What happened during those two years? A lot of new beginnings! I bought a house, this was always a dream of mine and I made it happen. That house, our home, was a new beginning. J and I found and started to attend a grief support, where I met Kim, who is now my best friend. Kim was a new beginning. I fell in love, it didn't last but it made me realize my heart is capable of loving again, while it ended it was still a new beginning, I just had to see it as such. I am making more room for love and less space for anger, for grief. Starting a blog, His Mom Strong, a new beginning...it only cemented what I already felt, healing is in helping. That's how I made it through the second February, helping.

God, very appropriately delivered a message of "presence" to me one Sunday in February. The sermon introduced the notion that we can't "fix" people or their problems, sometimes the best thing we can give to someone is our presence. I cried my way through the sermon (this isn't uncommon) because it hit so close to home. I thought so much about a friend who had lost her husband the month before. Had it not been for my own experience, I might not have agreed so much with the sermon, I might have been naiver to the topic. Maybe I would have tried to "fix her" or temporarily "cheer her up" and go on about my life feeling good that I had done something nice for someone. Maybe I wouldn't have understood what a long journey she faced, a very difficult journey. I learned the hard way that there is only so much I can do. We want so badly for our loved ones to be happy and whole, realizing we can't make them so, as badly as we want to is tremendously difficult, but there is power in knowing our limitations.

We can't heal people with scripture or platitudes, while they are always well intended and appreciated, we must dig deeper in caring for people. That might imply more work but sometimes the best thing we can say to someone who is hurting is nothing. Just be present. I realized what I could do. I realized what I felt was missing for me when I was grieving and I wanted to fill that gap. Enter my blog and reader feedback. Healing is in helping, I'm so thankful to be "His Mom Strong".

Life happens in 1,000 different ways, in 1,000 different spaces and no one is exempt from "life". Guess what? Sometimes life is hard. Life is not fair. Things happen that aren't supposed to happen. Whether it be a divorce, a job loss, a death, an illness, a stressful/overwhelming time in our life, we need people, people who will always offer us their presence. Presence is a present, it is a gift, a gift that is genuine, a gift that says you're not alone. This gift will never expire and it cannot be returned. It certainly can't be lost under a pile of condolence cards. No, I'm not suggesting we stop sending sentiments but that's not where we should stop either.

Moving on is difficult, but necessary. I have fought it kicking and screaming. I didn't know how to let go and to be honest I didn't want to. Holding onto my grief was holding on to Luke. If I stopped feeling constant pain, I stopped loving him, I would lose him again or more somehow, my pain kept him present. I thought letting go meant forgetting, I thought it meant moving on but I've learned there is a difference between moving on and moving forward. There is grace in letting go. I like to think I'm finally moving forward. A new beginning.

There is a great sense of relief in seeing how far I've come. As I sit here today, listening to the sounds of my life, I feel peace. My life could change tomorrow. What I have today might not be mine tomorrow, but in this moment, I love my life. I am happy and I feel peace. A new beginning.

I'm J's Mom, there is no greater title, no role I respect more and no bond I treasure more. Every day with him is a new beginning. Every day waking up to a blog I love, where people tell me I give them hope is a new beginning. Learning to love myself, to just be Stephanie, and not who I was all those years to Luke. Learning to see myself as I am and not how I felt he saw me.

To my son: J, I hope you remember the good & funny memories over the hard times. I hope you see that Mom tried to take advantage of every single "new beginning". I love you seems like such an incredible understatement, but Mom loves you so much, kiddo. Being your Mom is my greatest gift. You are my world, my strength, my greatest "new beginning".

To my family: I know I haven't always been easy to love. I know my pain sometimes made me difficult to recognize but you always saw me. Thank you for loving me through it all, for seeing me through and supporting all my new beginnings. You are my backbone, my lifeline and will always be home to me. I love you tremendously.

hismomstrong.com

Susan Rooks

How did I get started in the training business? Partly pure dumb luck and partly three total strangers who helped me become the Grammar Goddess.

It was 1995. I was unemployed (for the first time ever), looking in the Sunday want ads, and I noticed a really big ad from an international seminar company looking to hire the best and brightest speakers to lead seminars around the country. Paid speaking work. Auditions would be held in two weeks, and applicants were told to prepare an eight-minute business-oriented presentation. And we would be taped.

But I wasn't a speaker. Well, not in my book, anyway. I had been volunteering at a local teen drug rehab for five years, counseling (and attempting to calm) irate parents, many of whom were outraged at having to be a part of something because their kids had been doing drugs and were in the rehab. But the rehab's rules required everyone to learn more about drug abuse and recovery. The kids did not live at home for the first few months of their recovery program, and they couldn't be allowed to go back home if nothing changed there. Everyone who came into the home regularly had to go through some portion of the program, so they'd understand how to help the teen. Parents and siblings living in the home had to attend every week.

I was there two nights a week, and it was intense. I did stand and talk / coach / teach for about an hour each time, but . . . ?

Anyway, I was persuaded to audition. I prepared something lame, and showed up in Somerville, Mass., which is next to Boston, about an hour early because I wasn't sure where Somerville was.

STRANGER #1: THE INTERVIEWER
I was the only person in the waiting room, and eventually the interviewer came out and we talked for a bit. Chit-chatted. Schmoozed. He finally asked if I wanted to get my audition over with as no one else had shown up. YES! I did. I couldn't get it over fast enough. I was scared silly.

Afterwards, he and I talked a little more because whoever else was supposed to be there didn't show. I finally went home, sure that it had been a supreme waste of my time and his.

Surprise! A company rep called a couple of weeks later to say they liked my audition (I still wonder what it cost her to say that, because I've seen the tape). But Stranger #1 had labeled me "friendly and coachable." Bless his heart! I guess they figured they could teach me the skills I would need.

The rep wanted to know whether I'd like to start teaching computer skills or budgeting, the topics they most needed presenters for. I understood what she didn't say; those were the ONLY topics available right then. I knew nothing about computers, and since I'd majored in accounting in college, budgeting sounded less scary – and I really wanted the job! I paid dearly for that decision. Cue Stranger #2.

STRANGER #2: THE ANGRY MAN

On the morning of my second day "teaching" budgeting somewhere in Pennsylvania, an attendee stood and loudly proclaimed that I was the WORST presenter he had ever heard or seen, that I knew nothing about the topic (I had just said something backwards because I was so nervous), and that he was going to demand his money back! He then stalked out to stunned silence.

I called the company, told my "manager" I would finish out the two-week assignment, but never again. I refused to teach budgeting, and I was sure I would be let go. But, surprise! The company actually agreed to let me learn other topics (my guardian angel was working overtime that week!).

They offered me grammar (another topic no one else wanted), and that proved to be the right topic — eventually.

STRANGER #3: THE ENGLISH TEACHER

While I was more interested in learning to teach grammar than budgeting, I wasn't very good at it either, not at first. Few of us are brilliant in the early days, right? As they say, you don't know what you don't know — until you do.

But I enjoyed the work, didn't get yelled at, and I was feeling sure that I had made the right decision. Grammar was easy to teach!

So after about three months, when a nice woman came up to me at the end of the day, handed me her copy of the workbook, and mentioned that she had enjoyed my presentation, I was happy! She also said I might benefit from a couple of ideas she had, and she hoped I'd have time to look at the workbook and see her suggestions

But, of course I would! I beamed at her. What a lovely woman! I floated on air and appreciation.

I got to my hotel room and eagerly opened the workbook.

The workbook dripped red ink. Bled all over the place. Only a few pages didn't have red marks on them.

I was mortified! I had no idea I had made so many mistakes and obviously neither did my audiences for over three months. But she did. She was an English teacher, apparently a good one. And she was kind enough to sit through the whole day – I would not have been able to do that – and hand me her workbook, privately, with all her notes in RED ink, smiling all the way.

I have blessed her every day since.

So how did I finally become the Grammar Goddess?

First, there were those three strangers who propelled me in a direction I never imagined, to a goal I never knew I had. I wish they could just know how much they helped me even if that wasn't their intent.

Second, I finally had the right topic with the passion to do it correctly. I cared about the mistakes I made in the early months. I cared that I had given bad information. So I crawled all over the topic, rule by rule, page by page, until I knew the correct answers to just about anything a student could ask — at least in those seminars.

Third, there was my own need to excel. I refused to be less than the expert my students expected, and that's still true to this day. It still matters to me that so many business professionals — smart people— are confused about this foundation topic. And they're losing credibility as a result.

It still matters to me that they don't always know they've goofed.

It still matters to me that they don't always know whom to turn to for answers.

So I will keep on keepin' on, helping however I can.

I will continue to help business professionals look and sound as smart as they are.
Is there something I can help you with?

www.facebook.com/Grammar.Goddess
www.linkedin.com/in/susanrooks-the-grammar-goddess/
www.bebee.com/bee/susan-rooks
medium.com/@susanr_8577
twitter.com/Grammar_Goddess

TIFFANY BEVERLIN

Starting over, in one word "sucks". It seems to have even more negative connotations when starting over occurs after an unplanned life event such as divorce.

During my marriage, I worked hard, not outside the home, but in the home, raising three children all under six. I joke that this time I was in servitude to three children and one husband. The truth is in all humor there is an element of truth. My 16-year marriage had reinvented me from an independent career women to a stay at home Mom, who was totally financially dependent on their bread winning spouse. Along with losing my financial independence I also lost my identity, going from Tiffany, avid reader, fashion slave, fun, happy, adventurous traveler, to Mommy, someone's mom, someone's wife someone's daughter in law, sister in law. I barely recognized myself when I woke up to the sad yet long coming realization that my marriage was indeed over.

The first few months of divorce I fooled myself into thinking it really wasn't going to be that bad, that we would both just carry on as usual only in separate locations shuffling kids back and forth. I was almost shocked to realize that life was about to slam dunk me into a dark despair and unknown world of a single relationship status and no job prospects.

I often wallowed in the self-pity of despair those long months. I couldn't understand how if we both were married, we both divorced, how the outcome could be so financially skewed. I wanted to work, I needed to financially but also mentally. I was very ready to hang up my PTA crown, and put on my corporate suits again. Alas though, the corporate world really has no use or interest in a woman with a 12-year work gap in their resume. I felt such a mix of emotions, that somehow, I like many women, had been lied to re-having it all. It was instantly clear that making the choice to stay home, nurse, and raise my babies, had in fact taken away from me any chance of excelling in my chosen career. I was also now 16 years older and this didn't play well into the equation.

There is a funny thing about life, sometimes when you think everything is falling apart it is indeed falling together to take you to the place you need to be. My divorce was a prime example of this. I hadn't been able to sell my engagement ring, and after a fortuitous dream, I realized that I could sell my ring and the rings of all other divorcees on a website called DreamsRecycled. com. Making the one life time decision to follow that dream and start my company I knew nothing about, put me on a path that I am sure is in fact, my calling, to help other divorcees navigate divorce smarter and happier.

If I said this was an easy transition or a smooth ride I would be lying. Starting over after feeling like you had already been working your way to retirement and your kids all leaving for college, and being so close to that goal, was not simple. Recycling your life after divorce has many areas to attend to, recycling your career, your body, your identity, your relationships, your finances, are each in their own way a struggle. We want that easy button, we feel we deserve it, why do we have to go to the back of the line when we are so close to the front. The answer to this is, I really don't know why.

What I can tell you though is that in having a life event that forces you to start over, we are given a blessing, a blank sheet, a clean page in our book. All previous life choices in a way get erased. We may feel like we are at the bottom of the giant mountain of change, we get to pick, navigate, and conquer our own new personally chosen path to the top. Starting over allows us to make new dreams, new goals, and take new chances we never would have had the opportunity to take within a long-term marriage. We no longer must compromise except for our children. We can go anywhere, and do anything we choose to do. If you have nothing left, then you ironically have nothing left to lose. This too is a blessing as it removes some of the fear from our timid hearts that stop us from taking the kind of risks that in fact lead to bigger joy, bigger success, and bigger inner happiness.

You may find yourself like a fish out of water after divorce. You may feel like every thing is a loss, but I assure you if you start to focus on the things given as gains, and plan out your new life and goals, you will very soon start to not only accept change, but you will also start to be grateful for the redo button that has been placed in front of you by divorce. Starting over acknowledges the fact that you had to stop midway through something and go back to the beginning of a journey. Very quickly it equally reminds you that we live in a world of 7 billion people to meet, 206 countries to explore, and a million professional and personal choices in life that you get to make for you and no one else.

Tiffany Ann Beverlin
CEO founder Dreamsrecycled.com
Author My Dreams Recycled

https://www.facebook.com/dreamsrecycled
https://dreamsrecycled.com/
Twitter @Dreamsrecycled

MATILDA "TILLY" BEVERLIN

Starting Over

I was only 6 years old when my parents sat me and my two brothers down and told us that they would no longer be living together or married. At six, I really didn't understand what it all meant, but as time went on, I was about to start living two separate lives.

My biggest concern as a young child was about leaving my Mom, who had for my whole life been a stay at home Mom. I had never really spent time away from her except at school, and I became very anxious on weekends that I knew I was to stay at my Dads. My Dad had bought a new house in the next town away from us. My mom gave me her butterfly Betsey Johnson bag, as she knew I liked butterflies, to pack each weekend with clothes, toys, and my special elephant that I couldn't sleep without. It was very difficult for me. I would cry most Friday mornings and my Mom would get frustrated with me as we tried to get ready for school with me crying dramatically.

There was nothing wrong at my Dad's house, but the change and separation anxiety I had was normal for a lot of children adjusting to divorced parents. There were many changes. Not only did we have to sleep in a new house, but we had to get use to having two households with different routines, rules, food, and things to do in them. For example, my mom loves to cook, my Dad, though like many Dads, prefers simple quick and easy things to fix. My Dad's house was new so I didn't take many of my things there. I preferred to leave them at my Moms. My brothers seemed to adjust quicker to the two homes. They were older and loved the fact that there were no girly things to do there. My friends, too, had to adjust to playdates at my Dads. Mostly we would go swimming, and try not to get too loud.

When change happens and there is nothing you can do about it as a child, you must eventually accept it. Over time, the tears stopped, and the more of a reality it became -the more I chose to make the most of it. One thing that really helped was a year or so into the divorce, and when the anxiety I felt got too much, my Mom decided to buy us matching friendship bracelets. She told me that no matter how far apart we were, whether I was at Dads house or Timbuktu, that we were always attached by the invisible thread of love that runs between parents and their children. Love is the strongest of all emotions and cannot be altered by distance, change of circumstances, or divorce. I am 13 now, my Mom and I still wear the bracelets, which makes me feel better when she travels for work, or when I go somewhere with my Dad. Sometimes it is just something little that can make a difference to a child. My parents, I know, both love me unconditionally. Just because they parent differently or live in different houses will never change that. I think that is all children with divorced parents want, is to know they are loved.

Change is hard for children because we have no say in anything, but we are very adaptable over time to new situations, homes, schools, or even our parent's new partners. I think that it would be nice for my Mom and Dad to get remarried. I wouldn't even mind having step- siblings one day. That would mean starting over again, as a new kind of family, but I am ok with that too, as I have now realized I can cope with any change, and be happy with it.

As a child, I of course love that I get to have two birthdays, two Christmases, and two extended families that I get to see and spend time with. No child can be loved too much or by too many people. Now if only I could persuade my parents to buy me two kittens, I would be super happy.

My tip for anyone starting over would be to focus on the positive, and that having to begin again doesn't always have to be looked at as a bad thing.

Zac Halloran

I was supposed to be a teacher. I was supposed to teach history and coach my local high school baseball and basketball teams. I knew I wanted to make a difference in young lives by pursuing a career in education, but that all changed when my younger brother suffered a complex mental health disorder that left him in and out of the hospital for years.

Growing up with four brothers and two sisters was like being a part of a team. When my brother was faced with seemingly impossible odds, it was no surprise we all banded together to support him throughout his recovery. My family and I spent countless hours keeping my brother company and trying to make his stay at the rehab center as comfortable and familiar as possible. My mom would often make lasagna or other homemade meals to bring to my brother and the other individuals at the facility. The staff and other guests soon knew us all by name and smiled every time we visited.

After spending quite a bit of time there, I came to notice other individuals, a large portion of them being homeless, were not fortunate enough to have access to a safety net and love like my family provided for my brother. This sparked my interest in giving back and I knew a greater task was at hand for me. As my brother and I walked the halls of the rehab center, I wondered if there was a way to provide love and warmth to those in need right in our own community. It was then that I decided to put my career in education on hold to pursue a greater calling. Twill was born.

I chose to risk it all. I finished my masters at The College of Saint Rose, sold my car and began to go to work on my passion. After seeing firsthand the devastating effects of mental health illness in my hometown, I felt compelled to help lift the spirits of those in need. I believe the compassion I have for my family and community was the catalyst for my drive and desire to make Twill a reality. My basement became my office and sanctuary and I worked tirelessly to make this dream a reality. I had no business being in business. I had no background of business or marketing, but I understood people. I taught myself everything I could. From Photoshop to Facebook, I was now an entrepreneur with everything to gain.

I had to keep the lights on to keep burning the midnight oil. I needed to get a job that provided some flexibility during days. I couldn't have found a better place to work. I was hired as a Director at TSL Adventures, a before school, after school and summer program for school aged children. My bosses were very understanding of my schedule and truly loved the idea of Twill. These are the days entrepreneurs love to hate. From 6:30-8:30am I helped get the kids ready for their day and prepare them for their bus pick up. From 9am-1pm I had time to work on Twill, plan activities for after school and get whatever lunch I could. I spent most of my days either on the computer, phone or at meetings with potential clients. From 1:30pm-6pm I ran the after school program for about 40 kids and three staff members. From 6:30pm until I fell asleep at my desk, I was again working on my passion for Twill.

It was a very challenging time both for my career and personally. I often worked 90-100 hours a week and did so for three years. It was stressful, it took a toll on me physically and emotionally I was drained. I also was in a new relationship with the love of my life who lived in California. Yeah, I know I am crazy. We met at a dear friend's wedding in Rockport, Massachusetts and we would go back and forth from NY to LA monthly to see each other. So, I just started a business, I have a full time job, my girlfriend lives 3,000 miles away and my younger brother was in and out of the hospital and I only drank a cup of coffee a day. I honestly do not know how I had the strength left to carry on. I remember nights falling asleep on the phone with my girlfriend and being so physically and emotionally checked out.

I knew I couldn't go on this journey alone. I started reaching out for help. I asked my older brother, Jer, to join me. Jer would handle sales and the financial part of the business. He truly understood what I was trying to do and immediately lended a helping hand. Jer is responsible for helping to develop our Partnership Program. We needed to move faster and needed more hands on deck. An old friend and teammate from high school expressed interest in helping us with logistics and now Zach Hasselbarth is our Director of Operations and owns a portion of the company. We built great relationships with our local universities and added on bright, young interns who could help us navigate social media and events. We now have a growing team of talented marketers, event specialists and content creators.

In order to make any venture worthwhile and last, you must surround yourself with people who challenge you, who make you better and are positive influences on your mental and physical health. There are so many great people that have dedicated their time and energy to Twill over the years. Whether it be an internship or a short lived project, many have poured their heart into this company and helped me become a better leader along the way. The true key to being a leader is not telling people what to do, it is listening to your entrusted team members' feedback and make the necessary changes that are needed to be better than you were yesterday.

Playing sports has truly helped me understand the numbers game and the business arena. I played baseball in college and learned very quickly about competition and failure. I knew what my hitting percentage was, what my chances of success were and those numbers would only increase or decrease with more opportunities. It helped me put my business in perspective and inspired me to take more swings at creative ideas, talk to more people and learn how to handle failure along the way. I learned very early on in this venture that it is best to fail fast. It is good to take a chance on something you believe in. That campaign, idea or product you always wanted to put out there, do it! You will never know until you know. Maybe it doesn't work out, but what if it does? When starting up, it is cheaper to fail then rather than when you are already established. It is best to just go for it and learn as you go. Continue to take swings at new ideas, be creative and drive value for customers and your employees. You are going to make mistakes along the way, learn from them and quickly move on to the next at bat.

Lastly, I have learned to never rush something special. Twill began in my small basement apartment on one computer. Our goal is to make a difference in the lives of people who need it most. Providing a sample during a tough time can go a long way. I know firsthand how much a home cooked meal or a warm blanket means to a family member in need. It is through patience and perseverance that we have accomplished all that we have. We are like the little company that could, constantly chugging along to make it over the mountains. Every month we set a goal of how many people we think we could help, if successful, we celebrate by having a little pizza party. The little wins you gain while you're plugging along are like oxygen and help small businesses overcome obstacles. We needed every little win along the way. I depended on them.

Building something like a business with your heart and mind is such a fulfilling experience. Taking what was just an idea or a conversation to another level is not only difficult, but it seems impossible at first. I feel like an artist most times. I spend my days working on building out the company and connecting the dots along the way. Occasionally, I take a step back from it all and see the artwork revealed. I can see the amount of sweat and tears that it took to get where it is today. I can see the long hours of hard work from my team and I actually see them paying off right in front of me. It is now an organism with many different moving parts and people joining together as one unit.

Zac's brother, who became ill, has successfully completed his rehabilitation. He lives independently and helps at Twill events. Jer, is the CFO of Twill and manages a team of 10 at their local office. Zac lives in Los Angeles with his girlfriend Lauren and visits Albany every quarter. Zac focuses on national partnership and manages a small team in LA.

http://www.mytwill.com
hello@mytwill.com
@My_Twill
Facebook: Twill

The Second My Life Changed Forever

By AE on August 27, 2016: A wonderful book and inspiring author! Each story is an act of hope, courage, and incredible strength. The book is written with immense love and a testament to the human spirit! It gives each of us promise that even in the most difficult of times, there is hope .Thank you, Eileen Doyon, for the beautiful book and the wisdom and life lessons in your every chapter.

July 11, 2016: I really love the idea of so many short stories in one book. Real stories. It's gives the customer an opportunity to read many stories and gives everyone an opportunity to share theirs. Great job!

By B. S. Leidy on July 8, 2016: GREAT READ! Just got my copy today and I can't put it down! Anyone who has lived can appreciate the poignancy of the many stories of personal, and intimate, changes in life. I highly recommend this book!

July 28, 2016: I have now read three of Eileen's books and love them all! I usually read at night time and know I will be up extra late when I read her books. I keep wanting to read the next story and the next story and the next story! Thanks Eileen for inspiring us and sharing "real life" stories! I know this book just came out, but I'm already excited to hear what's next! If you haven't read any of Eileen's books, please do - you'll be glad you did!

By Edward Brewster on January 19, 2017: This is a must read for anyone who has enjoyed the Unforgettable Faces and Stories series by Eileen Doyon. This installment brings the reader back into the world of everyday people, and how life can change in a blink of an eye and how to adjust to those changes and come out on top. These are stories that will inspire and fill you with hope and inspiration. These are not made up or out of someones' imagination They are real. As real as the people who wrote them. I highly suggest this book and series as it will fill you with hope and love and maybe, just maybe they can help you find your way through the struggles of life.

July 6, 2016: Who doesn't need a bit of understanding and compassion as we deal with our daily struggles? This book keeps it real and exemplifies what it means to keep on livin' through all that we encounter. What a blessing!

By Jeanne Buesser on July 21, 2016: A must read! Eileen, I love the book. Your choices of stories are a really nice mix. It was inspiring reading all of them. When we go through hard times we all have to face our demons and not realize the strength we all have to be able to do it. Also that it is when we are in despair or at our lowest point is when the answers come the power to change ourselves and the direction. We may not realize this at that time, or get an aha moment until afterwards when we are able to breathe again,appreciating the opportunity afterwards in hindsight until much later.

July 6, 2016: It completely amazes me the struggles that we face can transform us to something incredibly great and we all have a true purpose. The book is truly inspirational. It completely amazes me the struggles that we face can transform us to something incredibly great and we all have a true purpose in life to inspire each other. I recommend this book to everyone to read especially those who are suffering in life, you can overcome it and inspire others yourself. A MUST READ!!!

By Cory B Houser on July 8, 2016: Eileen did an amazing job capturing the beauty and devastation in the world. People who's second changed them and made them do more good. People who's second opened their eyes and their hearts. This book is full of beauty and courage and love. Thank you for pulling so many of us together to share our second that it all changed.

July 7, 2016: Inspirational and Moving! Thank you so much to Eileen for including me in this book. Having the chance to read other people's experiences, was amazing for me as well. This book includes a lot of inspirational people and life-changing moments. I feel like, once you start reading, it pulls you in!

August 22, 2016: Inspiring. Read it all at once, or one inspiring story a day.... Gift this book to others and share the hope and wonder of these beautiful souls. Eileen did a fabulous job collaborating all these unforgettable true stories!

July 12, 2016: I love everything about this book! What a great idea to let people tell their own story, in their words! Amazing idea, great stories, inspiring people! Kudos Eileen!

By Carrie on June 23, 2016 ~ Inspiring!!!!

By Katy on July 12, 2016: This book is truly an inspiration! In a world of such tragedy, it is amazing to read how people have overcome any obstacle that has come their way.

July 6, 2016: I hope my story will inspire you. Inspiring, heartbreaking, failures, successes, love, passion, vulnerability and so much more. Must read. Buy one for you and gift one.

July 8, 2016: This book is a must have for anyone who has ever faced lose or the threat of losing someone. A Must Have Read! You wont regret it!

By DBB on July 24, 2016: Well done! So many great stories and so well told. Thank you, Eileen, for this literary contribution to the collective soul.

By Ken C. on June 25, 2016: Inspiring. An author that captures peoples amazing stories and inspires each of us.. Thank you for such a great book!

By MJC on July 8, 2016: Beautiful! Beautiful stories to uplift and encourage you. Thank you Eileen for such a wonderful collection!

July 12, 2016: A Heart-wrenching , triumphant, joyous and real roller coaster ride from beginning to end.

By AE on August 27, 2016: A Beautiful Book & One To Be Shared & Gifted. A wonderful book and inspiring author! Each story is a act of hope, courage, and incredible strength. The book is written with immense love and a testament to the human spirit! It gives each of us promise that even in the most difficult of times, there is hope .Thank you, Eileen Doyon, for the beautiful book and the wisdom and life lessons in your every chapter.

By Soulsis on July 3, 2016 Great book, uplifting! Good collection of stories to inspire and teach.

July 7, 2016: Just incredible! Just perfect life stories. Heartbreaking.

Letters To Heaven
By Mary Potter Kenyon on May 21, 2017
A wonderful compilation of letters to loved ones who died. A great idea
for anyone who wishes there was something they had said; write a letter to
your loved one. Then bury it in the cemetery, like I did, or burn it. Writing is
healing, either way.

By Julie Morse on June 20, 2017
These stories brought back feelings of the deep love I felt for relatives who
have moved on. Everyone has a story and these ones were told beautifully.

By M Hallon June 19, 2017
I highly recommend all of Eileen Doyon's books. Eileen is a breath of fresh
air. She is a very talented writer....we all have a story. I bought every single
book she has written.

*Please refer to Eileen Doyon's Author page on Amazon.com (www.amazon.
com/Eileen-Doyon/e/B00J8WTHW8) for additional reviews on all books*

Made in the USA
Las Vegas, NV
05 January 2022